Through the Lens of History

Through the Lens of History

Quinn Silver

CONTENTS

Chapter 1: Introduction

Overview of the JFK Assassination

The assassination of President John F. Kennedy stands as one of the most pivotal and shocking moments in American history. On November 22, 1963, the nation was abruptly plunged into mourning and confusion as news spread that the 35th President of the United States had been fatally shot while riding in an open-top motorcade through the streets of Dallas, Texas.

The day began with a sense of excitement and anticipation. President Kennedy, accompanied by First Lady Jacqueline Kennedy, had embarked on a political trip to Texas in an effort to mend frictions within the Democratic Party and to prepare for the upcoming 1964 presidential campaign. The weather in Dallas was clear and sunny—a perfect day for a parade.

As the presidential motorcade made its way through Dealey Plaza, the crowds lining the streets waved enthusiastically, eager to catch a glimpse of the charismatic young president and his elegant wife. At approximately 12:30 PM, the mood of the day took a dark and irreversible turn. A series of gunshots rang out, shattering the jubilant atmosphere and leaving onlookers in a state of shock.

President Kennedy was struck by two bullets—one in the upper back, exiting through his throat, and another fatal shot to the head.

Governor John Connally, who was seated in front of Kennedy, was also hit and severely wounded. The motorcade sped to Parkland Memorial Hospital, but despite the best efforts of the medical team, President Kennedy was pronounced dead at 1:00 PM.

The immediacy and brutality of the assassination left the nation reeling. Americans across the country gathered around their television sets, watching in stunned silence as the grim reality unfolded. The image of a blood-stained Jacqueline Kennedy standing beside Vice President Lyndon B. Johnson as he took the oath of office aboard Air Force One became an indelible symbol of the day's tragic events.

Within hours, law enforcement had identified and apprehended a suspect: Lee Harvey Oswald, a 24-year-old former Marine with a murky past and alleged communist sympathies. Oswald's arrest, however, did little to calm the swirling questions and fears. Two days later, Oswald himself was shot and killed by nightclub owner Jack Ruby, an act broadcast live on television and witnessed by millions.

In the days, weeks, and months that followed, the American public struggled to come to terms with the assassination and to make sense of the events that had transpired. The Warren Commission was established by President Johnson to investigate the assassination and to provide an official account of what had occurred. Yet, from the very beginning, doubts and suspicions lingered, giving rise to a multitude of alternative theories and the enduring mystery that continues to captivate and intrigue to this day.

This book embarks on a journey through the complex web of events, evidence, and speculation surrounding the assassination of John F. Kennedy. By examining the various narratives and theories, we seek to uncover the truth behind one of the most consequential and debated events in modern history.

The Official Narrative

Following the tragic events of November 22, 1963, the American government was swift in its efforts to provide clarity and calm to a nation in shock. Just days after President Kennedy's assassination, President Lyndon B. Johnson established the Warren Commission, named after its chairman, Chief Justice Earl Warren. The Commission was tasked with investigating the assassination and delivering a definitive account of what transpired on that fateful day.

The Warren Commission's final report, published in September 1964, concluded that Lee Harvey Oswald acted alone in the assassination of President Kennedy. The report meticulously detailed Oswald's life, actions, and alleged motives, painting him as a lone gunman with a troubled past. According to the Commission, Oswald fired three shots from the sixth floor of the Texas School Book Depository building. The first shot missed the motorcade entirely, the second struck both President Kennedy and Governor John Connally, and the third was the fatal shot that ended the president's life.

Central to the Warren Commission's findings was the "single bullet theory," also known as the "magic bullet theory." This theory posited that one bullet caused multiple injuries to both Kennedy and Connally, entering Kennedy's back, exiting through his throat, and then striking Connally in the back, wrist, and thigh. Despite the seemingly improbable trajectory, the Commission's forensic analysis supported this explanation, arguing that it was the only way to account for all the wounds with just three shots.

The Commission's report also addressed the role of Jack Ruby, who had famously shot and killed Oswald on live television just two days after Kennedy's assassination. The Commission concluded that Ruby acted alone and out of impulsive grief, dismissing any suggestion of a larger conspiracy involving Ruby's actions.

The Warren Report was intended to provide a clear and authoritative explanation of the assassination, and it initially succeeded in quelling some of the public's anxieties. However, from the outset, the report faced significant scrutiny and skepticism. Many Americans found it difficult to believe that a single, troubled individual could have altered the course of history so profoundly. The "single bullet theory," in particular, was met with widespread disbelief, earning its nickname as the "magic bullet" due to its seemingly implausible trajectory.

In addition to public skepticism, several members of the Warren Commission later expressed doubts about the completeness and accuracy of the report. Critics pointed to perceived gaps in the investigation, such as the failure to thoroughly explore Oswald's potential connections to intelligence agencies, organized crime, or other entities with a vested interest in Kennedy's death.

Despite these criticisms, the Warren Report remains the official account of the JFK assassination, and it has profoundly shaped the historical narrative. Yet, the enduring questions and doubts surrounding the report have fueled the rise of numerous alternative theories, each seeking to uncover the truth behind the assassination. The contradictions and mysteries highlighted by these theories will be the focus of the following chapters, as we delve deeper into one of the most enigmatic events in American history.

Emergence of Alternative Theories

From the moment the Warren Commission released its report, doubts about its findings began to emerge. While the Commission's conclusion—that Lee Harvey Oswald acted alone in assassinating President Kennedy—provided a sense of closure for some, it failed to satisfy a significant portion of the American public. The sheer improbability of the "single bullet theory" and the rapid succession of events that led to Oswald's death at the hands of Jack Ruby only added to the suspicion. These elements, combined with inconsistencies in eyewitness testimonies and physical evidence, laid fertile ground for the emergence of alternative theories.

In the years following the assassination, a variety of conspiracy theories have surfaced, each suggesting that the truth behind JFK's death is far more complex and sinister than the official narrative. One of the most persistent theories involves elements within the U.S. government itself. Proponents of this theory argue that powerful factions within the CIA, the military, or other government agencies saw Kennedy's policies as a threat to their interests. Kennedy's push for the withdrawal of American forces from Vietnam, his attempts to thaw Cold War tensions with the Soviet Union, and his stance against the proliferation of nuclear weapons are cited as potential motives for such a conspiracy.

Another major theory posits that organized crime played a central role in the assassination. During his tenure, President Kennedy, along with his brother Attorney General Robert F. Kennedy, had aggressively pursued anti-mafia initiatives. This crackdown on organized crime disrupted the interests of powerful mob leaders, leading some to believe that the Mafia orchestrated the assassination in retaliation. This theory suggests that figures within the Mafia may have collaborated with disgruntled elements in the government to carry out the plot.

The involvement of anti-Castro Cuban exiles is yet another significant theory. After the failed Bay of Pigs invasion, many anti-Castro militants felt betrayed by Kennedy's administration. These groups, backed by the CIA, had hoped to overthrow Fidel Castro and saw Kennedy's reluctance to provide full support as a betrayal. This theory posits that embittered anti-Castro militants, potentially with CIA support, sought to remove Kennedy to ensure a more aggressive stance against Cuba.

Beyond these major theories, numerous other possibilities have been suggested. These include the idea that international entities, such as the KGB, might have had a hand in the assassination, or that rogue elements within the FBI wanted Kennedy dead. Each theory attempts to address perceived gaps and inconsistencies in the official narrative, offering alternative explanations that range from the plausible to the outlandish.

The enduring appeal of these alternative theories lies in the unanswered questions and unresolved mysteries that continue to surround the JFK assassination. Why did the Warren Commission overlook certain pieces of evidence? Why were crucial documents withheld from the public for decades? Why did key witnesses change their testimonies or meet untimely deaths?

These questions, and the various theories they spawn, reflect a deep-seated mistrust in official accounts and a collective yearning to uncover what really happened on that tragic day in Dallas. As this book delves deeper into each theory, it aims to sift through the speculation and uncover the facts, providing a comprehensive examination of one of the most controversial and debated events in American history.

Chapter 2: The Historical Context

The Political Climate of the Early 1960s

The early 1960s were a period of intense political activity and global tension. The Cold War between the United States and the Soviet Union was at its peak, casting a long shadow over international relations and domestic policies. The threat of nuclear war loomed large, influencing decisions at the highest levels of government and creating an atmosphere of fear and suspicion.

President John F. Kennedy, elected in 1960, inherited a world fraught with challenges. His administration faced the daunting task of navigating the complex geopolitical landscape. One of the most significant events of his presidency was the Cuban Missile Crisis in October 1962. This 13-day confrontation between the United States and the Soviet Union over the presence of Soviet ballistic missiles in Cuba brought the world to the brink of nuclear war. Kennedy's handling of the crisis, which involved a naval blockade and intense negotiations, ultimately led to the removal of the missiles and a temporary easing of Cold War tensions. However, it also underscored the precarious nature of global politics during this era.

Domestically, Kennedy's administration was marked by a series of ambitious initiatives aimed at addressing social and economic issues. His New Frontier program sought to expand social welfare, improve education, and stimulate economic growth. These efforts were met with resistance from conservative factions within Congress, highlighting the deep political divisions of the time. Additionally, Kennedy's support for the civil rights movement, while earning him admiration from progressives, also garnered significant opposition from segregationists and other conservative groups.

The political climate of the early 1960s was further complicated by the ongoing conflict in Vietnam. Kennedy's administration increased American involvement in the region, providing military advisors and support to the South Vietnamese government in its fight against the communist North. This decision was driven by the broader Cold War strategy of containing communism, but it also set the stage for the later escalation of the Vietnam War under President Lyndon B. Johnson.

Kennedy's foreign policy decisions, particularly his stance on Vietnam and his efforts to improve relations with the Soviet Union, were not without controversy. Within the U.S. government, there were factions that viewed his approach as too conciliatory and feared that it would embolden America's adversaries. These internal divisions, coupled with the external pressures of the Cold War, created a volatile political environment.

In this context, Kennedy's assassination in November 1963 took on an even greater significance. It was not just the loss of a charismatic leader but also a pivotal moment in a period of profound political upheaval. The questions and theories that emerged in the wake of his death were, in many ways, a reflection of the broader anxieties and conflicts of the era. Understanding the political climate of the early 1960s is crucial to comprehending the myriad factors that may have contributed to the tragic events in Dallas and the subsequent controversies that have persisted for decades.

Social and Cultural Transformations

The early 1960s were a time of significant social and cultural transformation in the United States. This period saw the rise of movements and ideologies that would fundamentally alter the fabric of American society, setting the stage for decades of change and progress. Understanding these transformations is essential to comprehending the broader context in which President Kennedy operated and the challenges he faced.

One of the most prominent and impactful movements of the early 1960s was the civil rights movement. This movement, which sought to end racial segregation and discrimination against African Americans, gained significant momentum during Kennedy's presidency. Leaders like Martin Luther King Jr., Rosa Parks, and Malcolm X became household names as they led protests, marches, and boycotts to demand equal rights and justice. The fight for civil rights was marked by landmark events such as the Freedom Rides, the Birmingham campaign, and the March on Washington, where King delivered his iconic "I Have a Dream" speech.

President Kennedy's stance on civil rights was progressive for the time, but it also placed him at odds with many Southern politicians and constituents who fiercely opposed desegregation. Kennedy's administration took significant steps to support the civil rights movement, including the desegregation of public facilities and the protection of voting rights for African Americans. In June 1963, Kennedy delivered a historic address to the nation, calling civil rights a "moral issue" and advocating for comprehensive civil rights legislation. This bold stance earned him both admiration and animosity, further polarizing an already divided nation.

The early 1960s also saw the rise of youth culture and counterculture, which challenged traditional norms and authority. The post-World War II baby boom had resulted in a burgeoning population of young people who were eager to carve out their own identities and challenge the status quo. This generation, often referred to as the "baby boomers," embraced new forms of music, fashion, and social values that stood in stark contrast to those of their parents.

The counterculture movement, characterized by its opposition to the Vietnam War, rejection of materialism, and advocacy for social justice, began to take shape during Kennedy's presidency. The advent of rock and roll, the popularity of folk music, and the emergence of influential figures like Bob Dylan and the Beatles provided the soundtrack for a generation seeking change. This period also saw the rise of feminist and environmental movements, which would gain even more traction in the following decades.

Kennedy's administration recognized the importance of addressing the needs and aspirations of this burgeoning youth population. Initiatives such as the Peace Corps and the Space Race were aimed at inspiring and mobilizing young Americans to engage in public service and scientific exploration. However, these efforts were not without controversy. The generational divide created tension between the younger and older generations, with many young people viewing the government and traditional institutions with increasing skepticism.

The social and cultural transformations of the early 1960s created a backdrop of turbulence and dissent that significantly impacted the political landscape. Kennedy's progressive stances on civil rights, youth engagement, and international diplomacy endeared him to many but also alienated powerful groups resistant to change. Understanding these social dynamics is crucial to comprehending the complex interplay of forces that shaped Kennedy's presidency and, ultimately, the events leading to his assassination.

International Relations and Kennedy's Foreign Policy

During his tenure as President, John F. Kennedy faced a myriad of international challenges that tested his diplomatic acumen and strategic vision. The early 1960s were marked by significant geopolitical tension, primarily driven by the Cold War—a period of sustained political and military rivalry between the United States and the Soviet Union. Kennedy's foreign policy decisions not only shaped his presidency but also played a crucial role in the global perception of America's position on the world stage.

One of the most defining moments of Kennedy's presidency was the Cuban Missile Crisis in October 1962. This confrontation brought the world perilously close to nuclear war and tested the resolve of both the United States and the Soviet Union. The crisis began when American reconnaissance planes discovered Soviet ballistic missiles stationed in Cuba, just 90 miles from the U.S. mainland. The placement of these missiles was perceived as a direct threat to American national security, and Kennedy was faced with the daunting task of resolving the crisis without triggering a global conflict.

Kennedy's approach was a blend of firm resolve and cautious diplomacy. He opted for a naval blockade, termed a "quarantine," to prevent further Soviet shipments of military equipment to Cuba. At the same time, he engaged in intense back-channel negotiations with Soviet Premier Nikita Khrushchev. These efforts culminated in a tense standoff that was ultimately resolved when the Soviet Union agreed to dismantle the missile sites in exchange for a U.S. pledge not to invade Cuba and the secret removal of American missiles from Turkey. The resolution of the Cuban Missile Crisis was hailed as a significant victory for Kennedy, solidifying his reputation as a capable leader on the international stage. However, it also underscored the fragile nature of global peace during the Cold War era.

Another critical aspect of Kennedy's foreign policy was his approach to Vietnam. Kennedy inherited a complicated situation in

Southeast Asia, where the United States had been gradually increasing its support for the South Vietnamese government in its fight against the communist North. Kennedy escalated American involvement by sending military advisors and aid, a move aimed at containing the spread of communism—a cornerstone of the U.S. Cold War strategy known as the domino theory. Despite his intentions to prevent further escalation, Kennedy's policies laid the groundwork for the full-scale conflict that would later engulf Vietnam under his successor, Lyndon B. Johnson.

Kennedy's foreign policy was also marked by his efforts to improve relations with the Soviet Union and reduce the risk of nuclear confrontation. In 1963, the United States, the Soviet Union, and the United Kingdom signed the Partial Nuclear Test Ban Treaty, which prohibited nuclear tests in the atmosphere, outer space, and underwater. This treaty represented a significant step towards mitigating the nuclear arms race and showcased Kennedy's commitment to pursuing peace through diplomacy.

However, Kennedy's foreign policy initiatives were not without controversy. His decisions often put him at odds with powerful domestic and international interests. For example, his perceived leniency towards the Soviet Union and his handling of the Bay of Pigs invasion—a failed attempt to overthrow Cuban leader Fidel Castro—drew criticism from hawkish elements within the U.S. government and military. These factions viewed Kennedy as too soft on communism and saw his foreign policy as a threat to American dominance and security.

Understanding Kennedy's foreign policy and its impact on international relations is crucial to comprehending the broader context of his presidency. His efforts to navigate the complex web of global politics, while maintaining a focus on peace and diplomacy, reveal the challenges he faced and the potential sources of animosity against him. This backdrop of international tension and intrigue provides critical insights into the forces that may have contributed to the tragic events of November 22, 1963.

Chapter 3: The Official Narrative

The Role of Lee Harvey Oswald

Lee Harvey Oswald remains one of the most enigmatic figures in American history, his name forever linked to the tragic assassination of President John F. Kennedy. To understand the official narrative of the assassination, it is essential to delve into the life and actions of the man accused of this heinous crime.

Oswald was born on October 18, 1939, in New Orleans, Louisiana. His childhood was marked by instability and hardship. His father died before he was born, and his mother struggled to provide a stable home. Oswald's early life was characterized by frequent moves and a lack of consistent parental guidance. As a teenager, he became interested in Marxism and developed a fascination with the Soviet Union.

In 1956, at the age of seventeen, Oswald enlisted in the United States Marine Corps. His time in the Marines was marked by a troubled and contentious relationship with authority. Despite showing some aptitude for marksmanship, he struggled with discipline and eventually received a hardship discharge in 1959. Soon after, Oswald made a dramatic and unprecedented move—he defected to the Soviet Union.

Oswald's time in the Soviet Union was a key chapter in his life. He renounced his American citizenship and declared his allegiance to communism, but his experience in the USSR was far from ideal. He found life in the Soviet Union difficult and isolating. By 1962, disillusioned with his Soviet experience, Oswald returned to the United States with his Russian wife, Marina, and their young daughter.

Upon his return, Oswald continued to espouse pro-communist views and became increasingly vocal in his political beliefs. He moved to Dallas, Texas, and found employment at the Texas School Book Depository in October 1963. It was from this vantage point, according to the official narrative, that Oswald fired the shots that killed President Kennedy.

The evidence linking Oswald to the assassination was substantial. The rifle found on the sixth floor of the Book Depository was traced back to Oswald, who had purchased it under an alias. Eyewitnesses reported seeing a man in the sixth-floor window shortly before and during the shooting. Additionally, forensic analysis of the bullets and cartridges matched the rifle found at the scene. Oswald's fingerprints were discovered on the rifle and on boxes used to create a sniper's perch.

Despite the weight of this evidence, Oswald maintained his innocence. After his arrest, he repeatedly proclaimed, "I'm just a patsy," suggesting he was being set up to take the fall for a larger conspiracy. His assassination by nightclub owner Jack Ruby two days later, on November 24, 1963, deprived the nation of a trial that might have resolved some of the enduring questions.

The official narrative, as concluded by the Warren Commission, held that Oswald acted alone. However, the complexities of his background, his sudden move from defection to violent action, and his subsequent murder have fueled endless speculation and conspiracy theories. These doubts have kept the mystery of Kennedy's assassination alive in the public consciousness, as researchers and theorists continue to probe the life and actions of Lee Harvey Oswald, searching for a fuller understanding of his motives and the truth behind that fateful day in Dallas.

The Warren Commission Findings

In the wake of President John F. Kennedy's assassination, there was an urgent need for clarity and justice. To address the myriad questions and uncertainties surrounding the tragedy, President Lyndon B. Johnson established the Warren Commission on November 29, 1963. The Commission, named after its chairman, Chief Justice Earl Warren, was tasked with investigating the circumstances of the assassination and providing a comprehensive report to the American people.

The Warren Commission was composed of seven members, including prominent figures such as Senator Richard Russell, Senator John Sherman Cooper, Congressman Hale Boggs, Congressman Gerald Ford, Allen Dulles (former Director of the CIA), and John J. McCloy (a former Assistant Secretary of War and President of the World Bank). These individuals brought diverse perspectives and expertise to the investigation, which aimed to uncover the truth behind one of the most shocking events in American history.

Over the course of ten months, the Warren Commission conducted an exhaustive investigation. It reviewed thousands of documents, interviewed hundreds of witnesses, and meticulously examined the physical evidence related to the assassination. The Commission's final report, released in September 1964, concluded that Lee Harvey Oswald acted alone in the assassination of President Kennedy. This conclusion was based on a thorough analysis of the available evidence, which included forensic examinations, ballistics tests, and eyewitness testimonies.

One of the most controversial aspects of the Warren Commission's findings was the "single bullet theory," also known as the "magic bullet theory." According to this theory, a single bullet fired by Oswald from the sixth floor of the Texas School Book Depository passed through President Kennedy's neck and then struck Governor John Connally, who was seated in front of Kennedy. The bullet caused multiple wounds to both men before it was ultimately found on a stretcher at Parkland Memorial Hospital. The single bullet theory was essential to the Commission's conclusion that Oswald acted alone, as it accounted for all the injuries sustained by Kennedy and Connally with just three shots.

The Commission's report also addressed the subsequent murder of Oswald by Jack Ruby. On November 24, 1963, two days after the assassination, Oswald was being transferred from the Dallas Police Department to the county jail when Ruby, a local nightclub owner with alleged connections to organized crime, stepped forward and fatally shot him. The Warren Commission concluded that Ruby acted alone and out of a sense of outrage and grief, dismissing any suggestions of a larger conspiracy involving Ruby's actions.

Despite the thoroughness of the investigation, the Warren Commission's findings were met with skepticism from various quarters. Critics questioned the plausibility of the single bullet theory and raised concerns about the Commission's methodology. Some believed that the Commission had not fully explored Oswald's potential connections to intelligence agencies, organized crime, or other entities that might have had a motive to kill Kennedy. Additionally, there were claims that certain witnesses and pieces of evidence had been overlooked or inadequately examined.

The release of the Warren Report did little to dispel the doubts and suspicions that had already taken root in the public's mind. While some accepted the official narrative, others remained unconvinced, believing that a deeper conspiracy lay behind the assassination. The Warren Commission's findings, though intended to provide closure, ultimately gave rise to new questions and fueled the ongoing debate about the true circumstances of President Kennedy's death.

The Warren Report remains a pivotal document in the history of the JFK assassination. Its conclusions continue to be both defended and contested, as researchers and theorists scrutinize the evidence and seek to uncover additional truths. The Commission's work, while comprehensive, left an enduring legacy of controversy and intrigue that persists to this day.

Immediate Public Reactions

The assassination of President John F. Kennedy on November 22, 1963, was a national tragedy that reverberated around the world. The initial shock of the event was compounded by the stunning and chaotic developments that unfolded in its aftermath, capturing the hearts and minds of the American public and the international community.

In the hours following the assassination, the nation was plunged into a state of collective grief and disbelief. News of the President's death spread rapidly, with television and radio broadcasts providing continuous coverage of the tragic events. For many Americans, the moment they heard the news became an indelible memory—an emotional marker that would forever be associated with profound sorrow and a sense of loss. Schools, businesses, and government offices across the country came to a standstill as people gathered around television sets, radios, and newspapers to follow the unfolding story.

The immediate reaction to the assassination was one of shock and mourning. In Washington, D.C., a somber and respectful atmosphere took hold as government officials and members of Congress grappled with the enormity of the loss. World leaders expressed their condolences and solidarity with the United States, recognizing the profound impact of Kennedy's death on global affairs. Across the Atlantic, European capitals observed moments of silence and flags were flown at half-mast.

The events following Kennedy's assassination took another dramatic turn with the arrest of Lee Harvey Oswald, a former Marine and self-proclaimed Marxist, who was quickly identified as the prime suspect. Oswald's capture, however, did little to alleviate the public's unease. The chaotic circumstances of his arrest and the troubling questions about his motives and connections only deepened the sense of uncertainty.

Just two days later, the public was further stunned when Oswald was shot and killed by Jack Ruby, a local nightclub owner, in the basement of the Dallas police headquarters. This shocking event, broadcast live on national television, left the nation reeling once again. Ruby's actions eliminated the possibility of a public trial for Oswald, fueling speculation and conspiracy theories about the true nature of the assassination. Many questioned whether Oswald had acted alone or if there were larger, more sinister forces at play.

The release of the Warren Report in September 1964 sought to provide a definitive account of the assassination, concluding that Oswald acted alone. Yet, the report's findings were met with widespread skepticism. The "single bullet theory," a central component of the Commission's conclusions, was particularly contentious. Many found it difficult to accept that a single bullet could cause such extensive damage to both Kennedy and Governor John Connally. The term "magic bullet" became emblematic of the public's doubts.

Public reaction to the Warren Report was divided. Some accepted its findings and sought to move forward, while others remained convinced that the truth was far more complex. This skepticism was not limited to fringe elements; it permeated mainstream discourse, with respected journalists, scholars, and politicians expressing doubts about the official narrative. The burgeoning skepticism gave rise to a cottage industry of alternative theories and investigations, each attempting to uncover what many believed to be a deeper conspiracy.

The enduring impact of Kennedy's assassination and the subsequent reactions shaped American society in profound ways. The events of those days eroded public trust in government institutions and fostered a culture of questioning and cynicism. The assassination became a defining moment in American history, one that continues to evoke strong emotions and provoke intense debate.

As we delve further into the theories and evidence surrounding the JFK assassination, it is crucial to understand the immediate public reactions and the context in which they arose. The doubts and questions that emerged in the wake of Kennedy's death set the stage for decades of investigation and speculation, ensuring that the search for truth would continue long after the Warren Report was published.

Chapter 4: Lee Harvey Oswald's Background

Early Life and Ideological Development

Lee Harvey Oswald's life began in New Orleans, Louisiana, on October 18, 1939, in a family beset by adversity. His father died two months before he was born, leaving his mother, Marguerite, to raise him and his two older brothers in a succession of small apartments in various cities. This unstable and often turbulent upbringing had a profound impact on young Oswald, shaping his personality and outlook on life.

As a child, Oswald exhibited signs of intelligence and curiosity but struggled with social interactions and exhibited behavioral issues. His schooling was frequently interrupted by the family's moves, leading to a spotty educational record. Despite these challenges, Oswald developed a keen interest in politics and world affairs, often immersing himself in reading about historical events and ideological movements.

In 1956, at the age of seventeen, Oswald joined the United States Marine Corps. This decision was partly driven by a desire for stability and direction in his life. During his time in the Marines, Oswald underwent rigorous training and demonstrated an aptitude for marksmanship. However, his military career was marred by disciplinary issues, and he struggled to conform to the strict regimentation of military life.

It was during his service that Oswald's ideological leanings began to solidify. He became increasingly fascinated with Marxism and communism, frequently engaging in heated debates with his fellow Marines. His political beliefs set him apart and often made him a subject of suspicion and scrutiny within the military. Oswald's intense interest in communism culminated in a dramatic decision: in 1959, he defected to the Soviet Union, renouncing his American citizenship.

Oswald's defection was a bold move that drew significant attention. Upon arriving in Moscow, he declared his desire to become a Soviet citizen, though the Soviet authorities were initially wary of his intentions. Eventually, they allowed him to stay, and he was sent to Minsk, where he was given a job at a factory and provided with an apartment. Despite these accommodations, Oswald found life in the Soviet Union to be disillusioning. He struggled with the language, felt isolated, and became disenchanted with the reality of Soviet society.

In 1961, Oswald met and married Marina Prusakova, a young Russian woman. Their relationship added a new dimension to Oswald's life, but it did not dispel his growing dissatisfaction. By 1962, Oswald had decided to return to the United States, and with Marina and their infant daughter, he was granted repatriation. Upon their return, they settled in Texas, where Oswald continued to espouse his pro-communist views and became involved in various political activities.

Oswald's ideological journey was complex and marked by contradictions. He was a fervent believer in Marxist principles but often acted impulsively and erratically. His political activities included distributing pro-Castro leaflets in New Orleans and attempting to establish branches of the Fair Play for Cuba Committee. These actions brought him to the attention of both local authorities and federal agencies, further complicating his already convoluted narrative.

Understanding Oswald's early life and ideological development is crucial to comprehending his later actions. His journey from a troubled youth to a defector and then back to an alienated, politically active individual in the United States provides critical context for examining his motives and the events leading up to the assassination of President Kennedy. Oswald's story is one of contradictions and complexities, setting the stage for the many questions and theories that continue to surround his role in one of the most infamous events in American history.

Connections to Intelligence Agencies

One of the most intriguing and controversial aspects of Lee Harvey Oswald's life is his potential connections to various intelligence agencies. The circumstances of his defection to the Soviet Union, his return to the United States, and his activities in the years leading up to the assassination of President Kennedy have fueled speculation that Oswald was more than just a lone, disaffected individual.

Oswald's defection to the Soviet Union in 1959 raised many questions. At the height of the Cold War, defecting to the Soviet Union was an extraordinary and dangerous move. Oswald declared his intention to renounce his U.S. citizenship and offered to share military secrets with Soviet authorities. While the Soviets were initially suspicious of Oswald, they eventually allowed him to stay, providing him with a job and an apartment in Minsk. However, the KGB, the Soviet Union's primary security agency, kept him under surveillance throughout his stay.

Oswald's sudden return to the United States in 1962 further deepened the mystery. Despite his defection and public denunciation of the U.S., he was able to repatriate with relative ease, accompanied by his Russian wife Marina and their young daughter. The ease with which Oswald was able to secure his return raised eyebrows, particularly given the tense Cold War climate. Some researchers suggest that this unusual leniency could indicate that Oswald had connections with American intelligence agencies, such as the CIA or the FBI.

Evidence supporting this theory includes Oswald's interactions with various government entities after his return. For instance, Oswald made numerous visits to the FBI office in Dallas, ostensibly to discuss his efforts to establish a local chapter of the Fair Play for Cuba Committee, a pro-Castro organization. Some have speculated that these visits were part of a larger intelligence operation, suggesting that Oswald might have been an informant or agent provocateur tasked with infiltrating pro-Castro groups.

Furthermore, discrepancies and anomalies in Oswald's military records have led to questions about his true role. During his time in the Marine Corps, Oswald was stationed at Atsugi Air Base in Japan, a site known for its covert CIA operations. His duties included working as a radar operator, which would have given him access to sensitive information. Some researchers argue that Oswald's placement at Atsugi and subsequent activities suggest that he might have been recruited by intelligence agencies during his military service.

In addition to the CIA and FBI, there are theories that Oswald had connections to other intelligence networks. For instance, his brief sojourn in Mexico City in September 1963 has been the subject of much scrutiny. During this trip, Oswald visited both the Cuban and Soviet embassies, allegedly to secure a visa to travel to Cuba and the Soviet Union. The exact details of his activities in Mexico City remain murky, and there are conflicting reports about his interactions with embassy officials and intelligence officers. Some speculate that Oswald's trip was part of a larger intelligence operation, while others believe it was an attempt to defect again.

The complexities of Oswald's life and his potential connections to intelligence agencies add layers of intrigue to the story of the JFK assassination. While the Warren Commission concluded that Oswald acted alone, these connections raise the possibility of a more intricate and far-reaching conspiracy. Oswald's interactions with the CIA, FBI, and other entities continue to be a focal point for researchers and theorists seeking to understand the full scope of his involvement and the true nature of the forces behind the assassination of President Kennedy.

Anomalies and Inconsistencies in Oswald's Story

The story of Lee Harvey Oswald is riddled with anomalies and inconsistencies that have puzzled investigators and fueled numerous conspiracy theories over the years. From his movements on the day of the assassination to the conflicting testimonies of witnesses, these discrepancies cast doubt on the official narrative and suggest that there may be more to Oswald's role than meets the eye.

One of the most significant inconsistencies lies in the accounts of Oswald's whereabouts and actions on November 22, 1963. According to the Warren Commission, Oswald was positioned on the sixth floor of the Texas School Book Depository, where he fired the shots that killed President Kennedy. However, multiple witnesses reported seeing Oswald in different locations within the building around the time of the shooting. Some claimed to have seen him in the second-floor lunchroom just moments after the shots were fired, while others reported seeing a man resembling Oswald leaving the building immediately following the assassination.

These conflicting eyewitness accounts raise questions about Oswald's exact movements and whether he could have acted alone. The speed with which he allegedly moved from the sixth floor to the second-floor lunchroom, where he was encountered by police officer Marrion Baker, has been a point of contention. Critics argue that the timeline is implausible and suggest the possibility of another shooter or accomplice.

Another area of inconsistency involves the physical evidence. The rifle found on the sixth floor of the Depository was identified as the weapon used to kill President Kennedy. This rifle, a Mannlicher-Carcano, was linked to Oswald through purchase records and forensic analysis. However, doubts have been raised about the accuracy of the ballistic evidence and the chain of custody for the rifle. Some researchers have pointed out discrepancies in the handling and examination of the evidence, arguing that it may have been tampered with or planted to frame Oswald.

Additionally, the autopsy findings and medical evidence have been the subject of intense scrutiny. The Warren Commission concluded that Oswald fired three shots, with one missing the motorcade, one striking both Kennedy and Governor John Connally, and the fatal shot hitting Kennedy's head. This conclusion rests heavily on the "single bullet theory," which posits that one bullet caused multiple wounds to both Kennedy and Connally. Many experts and critics find this theory highly improbable, given the trajectory and damage attributed to the single bullet. The discrepancies in the autopsy reports, including conflicting descriptions of the wounds and the condition of the bullet, further complicate the narrative.

Oswald's personal relationships and activities also contain anomalies that have fueled conspiracy theories. For instance, his association with various individuals connected to intelligence agencies, anti-Castro groups, and organized crime has led some to speculate that he was part of a larger conspiracy. Oswald's connections to figures such as George de Mohrenschildt, a known CIA asset, and his interactions with Cuban exiles in New Orleans suggest that he may have been involved in covert operations or manipulated by more powerful forces.

Moreover, the behavior and statements of key witnesses have added to the confusion. Marina Oswald, Lee's widow, initially provided testimony that supported the lone gunman theory but later expressed doubts about his guilt. Other witnesses, such as Beverly Oliver and Jean Hill, have recounted seeing additional shooters or suspicious activity in Dealey Plaza, challenging the official version of events.

The anomalies and inconsistencies in Oswald's story highlight the complexities and unresolved questions surrounding the JFK assassination. These discrepancies have kept the debate alive and continue to inspire new investigations and theories. Understanding these inconsistencies is essential to gaining a fuller picture of the events leading up to and following the assassination, as well as the broader implications for American history and public trust in government institutions.

Chapter 5: The Zapruder Film and Physical Evidence

The Zapruder Film

The Zapruder film is perhaps the most famous and scrutinized piece of evidence from the assassination of President John F. Kennedy. Captured by Abraham Zapruder, a Dallas dress manufacturer, the film provides a harrowing and detailed visual record of the events that unfolded in Dealey Plaza on November 22, 1963. Its impact on public perception and the course of the investigation cannot be overstated.

Abraham Zapruder had brought his Bell & Howell 8mm movie camera to Dealey Plaza to film the presidential motorcade. Positioned on a concrete pedestal along Elm Street, Zapruder had an unobstructed view of the motorcade as it passed by. What began as a home movie capturing a moment of national pride quickly transformed into a historical document of profound significance. Zapruder's film, a silent recording running just over 26 seconds, captures the exact moment of the fatal shots that struck President Kennedy.

The film's significance lies in its ability to provide a real-time visual sequence of the assassination. It shows President Kennedy's limousine as it moves along Elm Street, the president and First Lady

Jackie Kennedy waving to the crowds. Suddenly, as the limousine passes the Texas School Book Depository, President Kennedy is struck by the first bullet, slumping forward in his seat. The film then captures the fatal headshot, graphically depicting the president's head snapping back and the subsequent chaos as the motorcade accelerates toward Parkland Memorial Hospital.

Upon realizing the importance of the footage, Zapruder sold the film to Life magazine for $150,000, a substantial sum at the time. Life published select frames from the film, but the full footage was not made widely available to the public until much later. This delay in the film's public release fueled speculation and conspiracy theories, as many believed there were details within the frames that contradicted the official narrative.

The Zapruder film has been analyzed exhaustively by investigators, researchers, and conspiracy theorists alike. It has played a crucial role in the examination of the trajectory of the bullets and the sequence of shots fired. One of the most debated aspects of the film is the moment of the fatal headshot, often referred to as the "head snap." Some analysts argue that the backward motion of President Kennedy's head suggests the presence of a second shooter from the front, potentially from the infamous "grassy knoll." This interpretation challenges the Warren Commission's conclusion that all shots were fired by Oswald from behind.

However, other experts have countered this theory by citing the phenomenon of the "jet effect," where the force of the bullet's impact causes a backward motion. Additionally, they argue that the film's frames support the single-bullet theory, showing the sequence in which Governor Connally is also struck.

The authenticity and completeness of the Zapruder film have also been subjects of contention. Some researchers claim the film was altered or tampered with before its public release. They point to alleged discrepancies in the film's frames and the timing of events as evidence of possible manipulation. Despite these claims, extensive forensic analysis has found no definitive proof of tampering, and the film is widely regarded as an accurate depiction of the events as they occurred.

The Zapruder film remains an iconic piece of evidence in the JFK assassination investigation. It has shaped public understanding and discourse, providing a visceral and unfiltered look at the tragic event. As we continue to explore the physical evidence, the film's role in supporting and challenging various interpretations highlights the complexities and enduring mysteries surrounding the assassination.

Ballistic Reports

The ballistic evidence from the assassination of President Kennedy is a cornerstone of the official investigation and has been the subject of extensive analysis and debate. The forensic examination of the bullets and cartridge cases recovered from the Texas School Book Depository and the presidential limousine plays a critical role in understanding the sequence of events that led to Kennedy's death.

The Warren Commission concluded that Lee Harvey Oswald fired three shots from the sixth floor of the Texas School Book Depository using a Mannlicher-Carcano rifle. According to the Commission, the first shot missed the motorcade entirely, the second struck both President Kennedy and Governor John Connally (the so-called "single bullet theory"), and the third was the fatal shot that struck Kennedy in the head.

The single bullet theory, which posits that one bullet caused multiple wounds to both Kennedy and Connally, has been one of the most contentious aspects of the Commission's findings. This theory relies heavily on the ballistic analysis of the bullet, designated as "CE 399," which was recovered from a stretcher at Parkland Memorial Hospital. Proponents of the single bullet theory argue that the bullet's relatively undamaged condition is consistent with its passage through soft tissue and bone, accounting for the injuries to both men. Critics, however, find the theory implausible, often referring to CE 399 as the "magic bullet" due to the improbability of its trajectory and condition.

Forensic experts conducted extensive tests on the Mannlicher-Carcano rifle and the bullets recovered from the scene. The ballistic analysis included comparing the markings on the bullets and cartridge cases to the rifle's barrel and firing mechanism. The results indicated that the markings were consistent with having been fired from Oswald's rifle, supporting the conclusion that it was the weapon used in the assassination. However, discrepancies and debates remain regarding the exact number of shots fired and the timing of those shots.

The condition and trajectory of the bullets have been subjects of intense scrutiny. The single bullet theory posits that the bullet entered Kennedy's upper back, exited through his throat, and then struck Connally, causing multiple injuries. This theory accounts for the alignment of the wounds and the location of the recovered bullet. However, some ballistic experts and researchers have challenged this explanation, arguing that the bullet's trajectory and damage are inconsistent with such a complex path. They suggest that additional shots or shooters may have been involved.

The analysis of the fatal headshot, often referred to as the "kill shot," also raises important questions. The Warren Commission concluded that this shot was fired from behind, based on the location of the wound and the direction of the bullet fragments. However, some researchers argue that the backward motion of Kennedy's head, captured in the Zapruder film, suggests a shot from the front, potentially indicating a second shooter. This interpretation has been supported by some forensic experts and remains a key point of contention in the debate over the assassination.

Another area of controversy involves the chain of custody and handling of the ballistic evidence. Critics have pointed to potential gaps and inconsistencies in the documentation and storage of the bullets and cartridge cases, raising questions about their integrity. These concerns have fueled speculation that the evidence may have been tampered with or planted to support the lone gunman theory.

The ballistic reports and forensic analysis of the bullets and cartridge cases are crucial to understanding the JFK assassination. They provide a scientific basis for the official narrative while also highlighting the complexities and uncertainties that continue to fuel debate. The differing interpretations of the ballistic evidence reflect the broader controversy and enduring mystery surrounding the assassination, as researchers and theorists continue to seek clarity and truth in one of the most pivotal events in American history.

The clock struck midnight, casting a silvery glow across the cobblestone streets of Seraphine. An eerie stillness blanketed the town, a stark contrast to the bustling chaos of the day. Only the distant hoot of an owl pierced the silence, like a lone sentinel guarding the secrets of the night.

In the heart of Seraphine, an old mansion stood imposingly, its weathered facade whispering tales of forgotten times. The mansion, known as Veilstone, was a relic of a bygone era, shrouded in mystery and intrigue. It was said that within its walls lay the answers to questions that had haunted generations.

Inside, the air was thick with anticipation. Candles flickered, casting dancing shadows that seemed to breathe life into the ancient tapestries adorning the walls. In the grand hall, a group of determined individuals gathered, their faces etched with resolve and curiosity.

Among them was Elara, a woman of fierce intellect and unyielding spirit. Her emerald eyes glimmered with a mixture of excitement and apprehension as she scanned the room. She had spent years unraveling the clues that had led her to this moment, and now, standing on the precipice of revelation, she could scarcely contain her emotions.

Beside her stood Kael, a seasoned historian with a penchant for uncovering hidden truths. His graying hair and weathered features bore testament to a life dedicated to the pursuit of knowledge. Kael's keen gaze met Elara's, a silent exchange of solidarity passing between them.

"Are you ready?" Kael's voice was a gentle rumble, a steady anchor in the storm of uncertainty.

Elara nodded, her determination unwavering. "It's time."

With measured steps, they approached the ornate pedestal at the center of the room. Upon it rested an intricately carved box, its surface adorned with symbols that seemed to pulse with an otherworldly energy. Elara's fingers trembled as she reached out, the weight of the moment pressing down on her.

As her hand made contact with the box, a soft hum resonated through the air. The room seemed to hold its breath, the very walls leaning in to witness the unveiling. With a deep breath, Elara lifted the lid, revealing a parchment that glowed with an ethereal light.

Kael leaned in, his eyes widening as he deciphered the ancient script. "This... this changes everything."

Elara's heart raced, her mind racing to comprehend the implications. The parchment held the key to a truth that had been buried for centuries, a revelation that would reshape their understanding of the world and their place within it.

As the night wore on, the group delved deeper into the secrets unveiled by the parchment. They unearthed tales of forgotten civilizations, lost treasures, and a destiny intertwined with the very fabric of existence. With each revelation, their resolve grew stronger, their purpose clearer.

In the quiet hours before dawn, as the first light of day began to chase away the shadows, Elara stood at the window, gazing out at the horizon. The journey ahead was fraught with challenges and uncertainties, but she knew they were ready. United by a common goal, bound by their shared quest for truth, they would face whatever lay ahead with unwavering determination.

The unveiling had set them on a path from which there was no turning back. And as the sun rose, casting its golden light upon the world, Elara felt a surge of hope and possibility. The future was a blank canvas, and together, they would paint a new destiny.

Chapter 6: The Conspiracies Begin

Initial Doubts and Public Reaction

In the immediate aftermath of President John F. Kennedy's assassination, the nation was plunged into a state of shock and mourning. The horrific event, broadcast across radio and television, left an indelible mark on the American psyche. The official announcement that Lee Harvey Oswald, acting alone, had assassinated the President did little to quell the growing tide of skepticism and doubt. Almost as soon as the initial shock began to subside, questions started to emerge about the true nature of the events in Dealey Plaza.

The first seeds of doubt were sown by the very nature of Oswald's arrest and subsequent murder. Oswald's background—his defection to the Soviet Union, his open Marxist beliefs, and his pro-Castro activities—seemed to make him an unlikely assassin driven by personal motive alone. When nightclub owner Jack Ruby fatally shot Oswald just two days after his arrest, on live television, it appeared to many as if the final chance for a clear understanding of the truth had been deliberately erased. Ruby's act fueled immediate suspicion that a larger conspiracy was at play.

Media coverage played a significant role in shaping and amplifying these doubts. In the days following the assassination, news outlets scrambled to provide minute-by-minute updates, often highlighting inconsistencies in official statements and eyewitness accounts. The sensational nature of the media's coverage not only kept the story in the public eye but also stoked the fires of speculation. Televised images of the shooting, repeated footage of the fatal headshot, and interviews with witnesses who provided conflicting reports all contributed to a growing narrative that there was more to the story than the public was being told.

Community forums, both formal and informal, became hotbeds of discussion and debate. In cities and towns across America, people gathered in living rooms, coffee shops, and local meeting halls to share their thoughts and theories. Letters to editors flooded newspapers, expressing frustration and suspicion about the official explanations provided by the Warren Commission. The advent of emerging online platforms in the years to come would only amplify these discussions, providing new arenas for conspiracy theories to thrive.

Specific cases began to gain prominence as more individuals came forward with their own doubts. Key witnesses, whose testimonies were either inconsistent with the official narrative or outright contradicted it, became focal points for conspiracy theorists. For example, several witnesses claimed to have seen or heard evidence of shots coming from the "grassy knoll" area in Dealey Plaza, suggesting the presence of a second shooter. These accounts were often dismissed or downplayed by official investigators but became crucial to the alternative theories that began to gain traction.

The initial public reaction to the assassination and the subsequent murder of Oswald created a fertile ground for conspiracy theories to flourish. As more people began to question the official narrative, the sense of doubt and mistrust deepened. This collective skepticism laid the foundation for the numerous conspiracy theories that would emerge over the following decades, each seeking to provide an alternative explanation for one of the most pivotal events in modern American history.

The next sections of this chapter will delve into the key figures who contributed to these theories and the alternative narratives they proposed, exploring how their work has influenced public perception and kept the debate alive. The initial doubts and reactions were just the beginning of a long and complex journey into the heart of one of America's greatest mysteries.

Key Figures and Their Contributions

As skepticism about the official narrative of President Kennedy's assassination grew, several key figures emerged who significantly contributed to the development and proliferation of conspiracy theories. These individuals, through their research, publications, and public statements, played critical roles in shaping the discourse and bringing attention to inconsistencies in the official account.

One of the most prominent figures in the early days of the conspiracy movement was Mark Lane, a lawyer and author whose 1966 book "Rush to Judgment" became a seminal work in the field. Lane meticulously examined the evidence presented by the Warren Commission, highlighting numerous inconsistencies and raising pointed questions about its conclusions. His legal background lent credibility to his arguments, and his book resonated with a public eager for alternative explanations. Lane's work inspired many other researchers and helped to establish the foundation for later conspiracy theories.

Another influential figure was Jim Garrison, the District Attorney of New Orleans, who became the only person to bring a criminal case in connection with the assassination. In 1967, Garrison charged New Orleans businessman Clay Shaw with conspiracy to assassinate President Kennedy. Although Shaw was eventually acquitted, Garrison's investigation brought significant attention to the possibility of a broader conspiracy involving multiple actors. Garrison's book, "On the Trail of the Assassins," published in 1988, further detailed his theories and became the basis for Oliver Stone's controversial 1991 film "JFK," which rekindled public interest in conspiracy theories.

Journalists also played a crucial role in uncovering and disseminating alternative narratives. Among them was Dorothy Kilgallen, a well-known columnist and television personality, who conducted her own investigation into the assassination. Kilgallen's articles challenged the official story and suggested that there were powerful forces at work to cover up the truth. Tragically, Kilgallen died under mysterious circumstances in 1965, fueling further speculation and suspicion among conspiracy theorists.

In the realm of literature, researchers like Harold Weisberg and Sylvia Meagher made significant contributions. Weisberg's book "Whitewash" and Meagher's "Accessories After the Fact" were among the earliest works to critically analyze the Warren Commission's findings. Both authors compiled extensive evidence and detailed their arguments with rigorous documentation, providing a scholarly foundation for the burgeoning conspiracy movement. Their work highlighted discrepancies in witness testimonies, forensic evidence, and the Commission's investigative process, reinforcing doubts about the official narrative.

Political figures also contributed to the discourse surrounding the assassination. Senator Richard Schweiker and Congressman Frank Church, both of whom were involved in congressional investigations during the 1970s, raised questions about the adequacy of the Warren Commission's work and the possibility of CIA involvement. Their efforts led to the establishment of the House Select Committee on Assassinations (HSCA) in 1976, which re-examined the evidence and ultimately concluded that there was a high probability of conspiracy, contradicting the lone gunman theory.

Activists and community leaders, such as Penn Jones Jr., a Texas newspaper editor, dedicated themselves to uncovering the truth. Jones meticulously documented the suspicious deaths of witnesses connected to the assassination, arguing that there was a systematic effort to silence those with knowledge of a conspiracy. His work further fueled public skepticism and kept the issue alive in the public consciousness.

These key figures, through their dedication and determination, significantly shaped the narrative surrounding the assassination of President Kennedy. Their contributions provided a counterbalance to the official account, encouraging ongoing investigation and debate. The legacy of their work endures, as new generations of researchers and theorists continue to seek answers to the enduring mysteries of that fateful day in Dallas.

Alternative Theories and Their Development

As doubts about the official narrative of President Kennedy's assassination began to surface, various alternative theories emerged, each proposing a different explanation for the tragic events of November 22, 1963. These theories ranged from the plausible to the highly speculative, but all shared a common belief: that there was more to the assassination than the Warren Commission's conclusion that Lee Harvey Oswald acted alone. The development of these theories was fueled by perceived inconsistencies in the evidence, conflicting eyewitness testimonies, and broader cultural and societal factors that made the public receptive to the idea of a conspiracy.

One of the earliest and most persistent theories involves the possibility of multiple shooters. This theory posits that additional gunmen, possibly positioned on the infamous "grassy knoll" in Dealey

Plaza, were involved in the assassination. Eyewitnesses at the scene reported hearing shots coming from directions other than the Texas School Book Depository and seeing suspicious figures in the area. The notion of a second shooter gained traction after the release of the Zapruder film, which some analysts interpreted as showing evidence of shots from different angles. This theory challenges the lone gunman conclusion and suggests a more complex and coordinated attack.

The "Magic Bullet Theory," or the single bullet theory, has also been a focal point for critics of the official narrative. According to the Warren Commission, one bullet—known as CE 399—caused multiple wounds to both President Kennedy and Governor John Connally. Skeptics argue that the trajectory and condition of CE 399 make this explanation highly improbable. Forensic analysis and ballistic tests have been used to both support and refute the single bullet theory, with no definitive consensus reached. The perceived implausibility of this theory has led many to believe that there must have been more than one shooter, each firing from different locations.

Another significant theory involves the potential involvement of the CIA and other intelligence agencies. Proponents of this theory argue that elements within the U.S. government had both the means and motive to orchestrate the assassination. The CIA, in particular, had a contentious relationship with Kennedy, especially following the failed Bay of Pigs invasion and his administration's push for rapprochement with the Soviet Union. Documents declassified over the years have revealed covert operations and internal discord within the agency, adding weight to the suspicion that rogue elements within the CIA might have been involved. This theory suggests that Oswald, a former Marine with known pro-communist sympathies, was either a patsy or a willing participant in a broader plot.

The Mafia, or organized crime syndicates, also feature prominently in several conspiracy theories. The Kennedy administration's crackdown on organized crime, led by Attorney General Robert F. Kennedy, angered powerful mob bosses. Figures such as Carlos Marcello and Santo Trafficante are often cited as having the motive to eliminate Kennedy as a way to protect their interests. Theories involving the Mafia often suggest a collaboration between organized crime and rogue elements of the government, uniting their resources to carry out the assassination and subsequent cover-up.

These alternative theories have been further developed and propagated through the work of independent researchers, investigative journalists, and popular media. Books, documentaries, and films have explored various aspects of the assassination, often presenting new evidence or interpretations that challenge the official story. The advent of the internet has provided a platform for a vast array of voices, making it easier for conspiracy theories to spread and gain traction among the public.

Cultural and societal factors have also played a significant role in the development of these theories. The 1960s were a time of significant social upheaval and distrust of authority. The Vietnam War, the civil rights movement, and high-profile political scandals such as Watergate eroded public trust in government institutions. This climate of suspicion made the public more receptive to alternative explanations for Kennedy's assassination, viewing it as part of a broader pattern of deceit and corruption.

As we delve deeper into the specific theories and their proponents in the following chapters, it is essential to understand the broader context in which these alternative narratives emerged. The development of these theories reflects a complex interplay of evidence, interpretation, and cultural dynamics, ensuring that the mystery of the JFK assassination remains a topic of enduring fascination and debate.

Chapter 7: Government Involvement Theories

CIA's Distrust and Alleged Motives
The Central Intelligence Agency (CIA) played a pivotal role in the fabric of American governance and international relations during the Cold War. Its vast network of operatives and covert operations spanned the globe, influencing foreign and domestic policy in profound ways. President John F. Kennedy's relationship with the CIA was complex and fraught with tension, marked by a series of conflicts and disagreements that some believe culminated in his assassination.

The first major rift between Kennedy and the CIA occurred in the aftermath of the Bay of Pigs invasion in April 1961. The failed attempt to overthrow Cuban leader Fidel Castro was a disaster, resulting in the capture or death of many anti-Castro exiles and a humiliating defeat for the United States. Kennedy, who had reluctantly approved the operation based on the CIA's assurances of success, felt betrayed by the agency's poor planning and execution. The debacle severely damaged Kennedy's trust in the CIA and led to significant changes within the agency. He forced the resignation of CIA Director Allen Dulles, along with other top officials, and vowed to curtail the agency's power, famously expressing his desire to "splinter the CIA into a thousand pieces and scatter it to the winds."

Kennedy's determination to limit the CIA's influence extended to his broader foreign policy agenda. He sought to reduce the agency's involvement in covert operations and intelligence-gathering, particularly in Latin America and Southeast Asia. This shift in policy was met with resistance from within the CIA, where many operatives viewed Kennedy's actions as a threat to their mission and the nation's security. The agency's deep-seated culture of autonomy and secrecy clashed with Kennedy's vision of a more transparent and accountable intelligence apparatus.

Further exacerbating the tension was Kennedy's approach to the Cold War. While the president maintained a firm stance against communism, he also pursued diplomatic efforts to reduce tensions with the Soviet Union. His administration's push for the Nuclear Test Ban Treaty and his famous "Ich bin ein Berliner" speech in West Berlin signaled a willingness to engage in dialogue with America's adversaries. This approach was at odds with the CIA's more aggressive stance, which favored covert actions and regime change to combat communist influence.

One of the most significant sources of friction between Kennedy and the CIA was his administration's evolving policy on Vietnam. Initially, Kennedy increased American military aid and advisors to South Vietnam as part of the effort to contain communism. However, as the situation in Vietnam deteriorated, Kennedy began to reconsider the wisdom of deepening U.S. involvement. He privately expressed doubts about the viability of a military solution and hinted at plans to withdraw American forces after the 1964 election. This shift alarmed the military-industrial complex and hawkish elements within the CIA, who viewed a strong U.S. presence in Vietnam as essential to countering Soviet influence in Southeast Asia.

These cumulative factors created an environment of distrust and resentment within the CIA toward Kennedy. The agency's operatives, many of whom were fiercely anti-communist and deeply committed to their mission, saw Kennedy's actions as not only undermining their efforts but also jeopardizing national security. The idea that elements within the CIA might have viewed Kennedy as a threat to be eliminated is not without precedent; the agency had been involved in numerous covert operations to overthrow foreign leaders perceived as hostile to U.S. interests.

As we delve deeper into the theories surrounding government involvement in Kennedy's assassination, the alleged motives and actions of the CIA will be a central focus. The complex and often contentious relationship between the president and the agency provides a crucial backdrop for understanding the broader context in which these theories emerged.

Military and Defense Department's Involvement

The notion that elements of the U.S. military and the Department of Defense (DoD) might have played a role in the assassination of President John F. Kennedy is one that has garnered significant attention and speculation. This theory hinges on the premise that Kennedy's policies and actions threatened the interests of the military-industrial complex—a powerful alliance between the armed forces and defense contractors that President Dwight D. Eisenhower famously warned about in his farewell address.

One of the key factors that fueled suspicion of military involvement was Kennedy's evolving stance on Vietnam. Initially, Kennedy had increased American military aid and advisors to support the South Vietnamese government against the communist North. This policy was in line with the broader Cold War strategy of containing communism. However, as the situation in Vietnam deteriorated and the costs—both human and financial—began to mount, Kennedy started to reconsider the extent of U.S. involvement. In the months leading up to his assassination, Kennedy had privately expressed doubts about the viability of a military solution in Vietnam and hinted at plans to withdraw American forces after the 1964 election.

This potential shift in policy was alarming to many within the military establishment and defense contractors who stood to gain from continued military engagement. The prospect of scaling back the U.S. presence in Vietnam threatened the interests of those who were deeply invested in the conflict, both ideologically and financially. The military-industrial complex had become a significant force in American politics, with substantial influence over policy decisions and a vested interest in maintaining a strong military posture.

Kennedy's commitment to pursuing diplomatic solutions and de-escalation was evident in his broader foreign policy agenda. His administration's efforts to improve relations with the Soviet Union, culminating in the signing of the Partial Nuclear Test Ban Treaty in 1963, reflected a desire to reduce the risk of nuclear confrontation and promote peaceful coexistence. This approach was in stark contrast to the more hawkish elements within the military and defense sectors, who viewed the Soviet Union as an implacable enemy that required a robust military response.

The president's speeches and public statements also underscored his concerns about the influence of the military-industrial complex. In his famous address at American University in June 1963, Kennedy spoke of the need for a "strategy of peace" and emphasized the importance of diplomacy and mutual understanding between nations. His call for a reassessment of national priorities and the reduction of military expenditures was seen by many as a direct challenge to the entrenched interests of the defense establishment.

These tensions were further exacerbated by Kennedy's efforts to assert civilian control over the military. His insistence on being involved in strategic decisions and his skepticism of military advice led to clashes with top generals and defense officials. Some in the military perceived Kennedy as inexperienced and naive, a president who did not fully grasp the complexities of global power dynamics and the necessity of maintaining military strength.

The combination of Kennedy's perceived threat to the status quo, his plans for a potential withdrawal from Vietnam, and his broader push for peaceful coexistence with the Soviet Union created an environment of deep mistrust and animosity. In this context, it is not difficult to see how some theorists have posited that elements within the military and defense sectors might have seen the assassination of Kennedy as a necessary action to preserve their interests and maintain American hegemony.

As we explore further, the evidence and testimonies that suggest possible government involvement in the assassination will be crucial in understanding the broader implications of these theories. The complex interplay of politics, power, and ideology during this turbulent period provides a fertile ground for speculation and continued investigation into one of the most controversial and debated events in American history.

Actions and Evidence Supporting Government Involvement

The possibility of U.S. government involvement in the assassination of President John F. Kennedy is supported by various actions and pieces of evidence that suggest a concerted effort to cover up the true nature of the events. These elements, while not providing definitive proof, raise significant questions and fuel the ongoing debate about the role of government agencies in the assassination.

One of the most suspicious actions following the assassination was the rapid destruction and suppression of crucial documents and evidence. Key pieces of evidence, such as the original autopsy photographs and X-rays, have either been lost or are missing. This loss has made it difficult for independent investigators to verify the findings of the Warren Commission. Additionally, the notes taken by Dr. Malcolm Perry, the surgeon who tried to save President Kennedy at Parkland Memorial Hospital, were reportedly confiscated and never seen again. Such actions have led to speculation that evidence was deliberately destroyed to prevent a thorough and transparent investigation.

Another critical point of contention is the behavior of certain individuals and agencies immediately following the assassination. The quick conclusion by the FBI that Oswald was the lone assassin, without thoroughly investigating alternative theories, has been cited as suspicious. J. Edgar Hoover, the FBI Director at the time, was known for his fierce protection of the Bureau's reputation and his animosity toward the Kennedy administration. Hoover's apparent eagerness to close the case swiftly and his dismissal of dissenting voices within the FBI suggest a possible motive to suppress information that could implicate other parties.

The involvement of the Secret Service on the day of the assassination has also been scrutinized. Critics argue that the Secret Service's actions and inactions contributed to Kennedy's vulnerability. For example, the decision to change the motorcade route and the lack of Secret Service agents positioned on the running boards of the presidential limousine were highly unusual. Additionally, reports of agents being out late the night before the assassination, which could have impaired their performance, further cast doubt on the level of protection provided. Some conspiracy theorists posit that these lapses were not merely coincidental but part of a deliberate plan to facilitate the assassination.

Testimonies from whistleblowers and former government officials have also added fuel to the conspiracy theories. E. Howard

Hunt, a former CIA officer involved in covert operations, claimed before his death that he had knowledge of a conspiracy to kill Kennedy. Hunt's assertions, although contested and lacking concrete evidence, suggest that there were individuals within the intelligence community who believed in or had knowledge of a larger plot. Similarly, other former officials and operatives have come forward with stories of suspicious activities and conversations that imply a cover-up.

The mysterious deaths of several witnesses connected to the assassination have further deepened the suspicion of a government conspiracy. Over the years, numerous individuals who claimed to have seen or heard crucial information about the assassination have died under questionable circumstances. While some of these deaths can be attributed to natural causes or accidents, the sheer number of such cases has led many to believe that a concerted effort was made to silence those who could expose the truth. This phenomenon, often referred to as the "Witness Deaths," has become a central pillar in many conspiracy theories.

Finally, the release of classified documents over the years has provided new insights and reignited debates. While many documents remain heavily redacted or classified, those that have been released reveal inconsistencies and omissions in the official narrative. The continued reluctance of government agencies to fully declassify all related documents only adds to the suspicion that there is something to hide.

The actions and evidence supporting theories of government involvement in Kennedy's assassination paint a complex and troubling picture. While definitive proof remains elusive, the accumulation of suspicious activities, missing evidence, and testimonies from insiders suggest that the true story of what happened on November 22, 1963, is far more complicated than the official account. As researchers and theorists continue to dig deeper, the quest for truth remains a testament to the enduring mystery and controversy surrounding one of America's darkest days.

| 54 | – CHAPTER 7: GOVERNMENT INVOLVEMENT THEORIES

Chapter 8: The Mafia Connection

Potential Motives of the Mafia

The assassination of President John F. Kennedy is a mystery steeped in a web of potential conspiracies, and one of the most compelling theories points to the involvement of the Mafia. The relationship between the Kennedy administration and organized crime was complex and fraught with tension, particularly due to the aggressive crackdown on the Mafia led by Attorney General Robert F. Kennedy. This campaign of relentless legal action and investigation posed a significant threat to the power and prosperity of key Mafia figures, providing a strong motive for their potential involvement in the assassination.

Robert F. Kennedy's war on organized crime was unprecedented in its scope and intensity. Upon taking office, he made it clear that dismantling the Mafia was a top priority for the Justice Department. He established the Organized Crime Section within the Justice Department and significantly increased the number of federal prosecutions against mob figures. High-profile investigations and indictments became common, with the Kennedys making enemies among the nation's most powerful crime families.

One of the primary targets of the Kennedy administration's crackdown was Carlos Marcello, the reputed boss of the New Orleans crime family. Marcello, whose empire spanned much of the southeastern United States, was known for his involvement in various illegal activities, including racketeering, extortion, and drug trafficking. In 1961, Robert Kennedy orchestrated Marcello's deportation to Guatemala in a dramatic and controversial move. Although Marcello soon returned to the United States, the incident left him with a deep and personal grudge against the Kennedy family. Some researchers believe that this vendetta could have provided Marcello with a powerful motive to orchestrate or support an assassination plot.

Another key figure who felt the heat from the Kennedys' crackdown was Sam Giancana, the boss of the Chicago Outfit. Giancana's operations extended into Las Vegas, where he controlled significant interests in the burgeoning casino industry. The Kennedys' aggressive stance on organized crime threatened to disrupt these lucrative ventures. Furthermore, Giancana reportedly had a personal connection to the Kennedy family through his romantic involvement with Judith Exner, who was also rumored to be an associate of President Kennedy. This intertwining of personal and professional relationships adds a layer of intrigue to the theory that Giancana could have had motives to eliminate the President.

Santo Trafficante Jr., the powerful boss of the Tampa crime family, also had reasons to resent the Kennedy administration. Trafficante's operations included significant investments in Cuban casinos, which suffered greatly after Fidel Castro's rise to power and subsequent nationalization of the gaming industry. The failed Bay of Pigs invasion and the Kennedy administration's strained relations with Cuba further complicated Trafficante's business interests. Some theories suggest that Trafficante, like Marcello and Giancana, saw the assassination of Kennedy as a means to protect and advance his criminal empire.

The collective interests of these powerful Mafia figures, coupled with their personal vendettas and financial stakes, created a plausible motive for their involvement in the assassination. The Kennedys' crackdown on organized crime threatened not only the financial stability of these crime families but also their very survival. In a world where power struggles and vendettas often led to violence, the assassination of President Kennedy could be seen as a strategic move to eliminate a formidable adversary.

As we delve deeper into this theory, the following sections will examine the evidence and connections that suggest Mafia involvement, as well as the role of Jack Ruby in potentially silencing Lee Harvey Oswald. Understanding the motives behind the Mafia's animosity toward the Kennedys is crucial to piecing together the larger puzzle of this enduring mystery.

Evidence of Mafia Involvement

While the potential motives of the Mafia to assassinate President John F. Kennedy are compelling, any serious investigation must also consider the evidence that supports these claims. Over the years, numerous pieces of evidence have surfaced, ranging from testimonies of mob informants to suspicious activities and connections between key figures. Although definitive proof remains elusive, the accumulation of these pieces provides a compelling argument for the Mafia's involvement.

One significant source of evidence comes from mob informants and associates who have come forward with information suggesting a Mafia role in the assassination. Among the most notable was Johnny Roselli, a high-ranking member of the Chicago Outfit. Roselli testified before the Senate Select Committee on Intelligence in the 1970s, where he hinted at Mafia involvement in the assassination. He claimed that the Mafia had been angered by the Kennedys' crackdown and had collaborated with rogue CIA operatives to eliminate the President. While some skeptics argue that Roselli's statements were self-serving and lacked concrete evidence, they nonetheless provided valuable insight into the possible collusion between organized crime and elements within the government.

Additionally, links between Lee Harvey Oswald and figures within the Mafia have been scrutinized. Jack Ruby, the nightclub owner who killed Oswald, had well-documented connections to organized crime. Ruby's frequent interactions with known mob figures, including Carlos Marcello's associates, suggest that he was more than a simple nightclub owner with a patriotic motive to kill Oswald. Some theories propose that Ruby was instructed by the Mafia to silence Oswald, preventing him from potentially revealing information that could implicate a broader conspiracy. Ruby's own behavior and statements after his arrest, including his claims that he acted on behalf of "higher-ups," have been interpreted by some as evidence of a larger plot.

Further bolstering the case for Mafia involvement are suspicious activities observed in the days leading up to the assassination. For instance, David Ferrie, a pilot and associate of both Carlos Marcello and Lee Harvey Oswald, was implicated in several conspiracy theories. Ferrie's abrupt and suspicious behavior following the assassination, including his immediate departure from New Orleans and subsequent mysterious death, has raised questions about his potential role in the events. Ferrie was later portrayed as a key figure in Jim Garrison's investigation into the assassination, and his connections to both the Mafia and Oswald continue to fuel speculation.

The House Select Committee on Assassinations (HSCA), which reinvestigated the Kennedy assassination in the late 1970s, also found evidence that supported the theory of Mafia involvement.

The HSCA concluded that there was a "high probability" of a conspiracy, noting the potential role of organized crime in the assassination. The committee's findings were based on a review of the evidence, including wiretapped conversations of mob leaders discussing their animosity toward the Kennedys and the potential benefits of removing the President from power.

Lastly, the unexplained deaths of several individuals connected to the assassination have fueled suspicions of a cover-up. Witnesses who claimed to have information about Mafia involvement, including Roselli, Sam Giancana, and David Ferrie, died under suspicious circumstances. These deaths, often occurring just before they were scheduled to testify or provide crucial information, have led some to believe that a systematic effort was made to silence those who might reveal the truth.

The evidence supporting the theory of Mafia involvement in the assassination of President Kennedy is extensive and multifaceted. While it may not provide definitive proof, the combination of informant testimonies, connections between key figures, and suspicious activities creates a compelling narrative. As we continue to explore this theory, the role of Jack Ruby will be examined in greater detail, shedding light on his possible connections to the Mafia and his actions in the aftermath of the assassination.

Chapter 9: The Role of Anti-Castro Cubans

Connections to Lee Harvey Oswald

The intriguing web of connections between Lee Harvey Oswald and anti-Castro Cuban exiles adds a fascinating layer to the complex narrative of President John F. Kennedy's assassination. To fully understand this, it's crucial to delve into Oswald's known interactions and associations with various Cuban exile groups and individuals who were vehemently opposed to Fidel Castro's regime.

One of the most notable connections is Oswald's purported visit to Silvia Odio, a Cuban exile living in Dallas. In late September 1963, just a few weeks before the assassination, Odio claimed that Oswald, accompanied by two other men, visited her apartment. According to Odio, these men introduced Oswald as "Leon Oswald" and described him as an ex-Marine who was deeply committed to the Cuban cause. Odio later testified that one of the men told her that Oswald was "kind of loco" and capable of killing. This encounter, if true, places Oswald in direct contact with anti-Castro elements and suggests that he might have been involved in or manipulated by these groups.

Oswald's political activities also provide a glimpse into his complex relationship with Cuban exile groups. Despite publicly presenting himself as a pro-Castro activist, Oswald's actions were often contradictory and confusing. He was the self-proclaimed secretary of the New Orleans chapter of the Fair Play for Cuba Committee (FPCC), a pro-Castro organization. Oswald's public demonstrations and distribution of pro-Castro literature put him in direct opposition to anti-Castro Cuban exiles, yet there were instances that hinted at a deeper, covert relationship.

For example, Oswald's attempts to infiltrate anti-Castro organizations, such as the Cuban Revolutionary Council, raise questions about his true loyalties and intentions. He sought out interactions with these groups, which could suggest that he was trying to gather intelligence or disrupt their activities. Alternatively, some theorists propose that Oswald's pro-Castro persona was a facade to cover his true role as an agent provocateur, working on behalf of U.S. intelligence agencies or even the anti-Castro Cubans themselves.

The connection between Oswald and anti-Castro Cubans extends beyond individual interactions. His time in Mexico City in late September 1963, where he visited the Cuban and Soviet embassies, further complicates the narrative. While the details of his activities in Mexico City remain murky, some reports suggest that Oswald was seeking a visa to travel to Cuba and possibly the Soviet Union. This period has been the subject of intense scrutiny, with various theories proposing that Oswald was either seeking support for an assassination plot or attempting to defect.

Moreover, the broader context of U.S.-Cuban relations during this period adds another layer of complexity. The failed Bay of Pigs invasion in April 1961 had left deep scars and a sense of betrayal among Cuban exiles who felt abandoned by the Kennedy administration. This betrayal fueled a burning hatred towards Kennedy, which could have driven some exiles to seek vengeance. The possibility that anti-Castro Cubans saw in Oswald a willing participant or a useful pawn in a larger conspiracy cannot be discounted.

In summary, the connections between Lee Harvey Oswald and anti-Castro Cuban exiles are a critical piece of the puzzle in understanding the assassination of President Kennedy. These interactions highlight the intricate and often contradictory web of relationships that defined Oswald's life and actions in the months leading up to the tragic event in Dallas. As we continue to explore this theory, the motives and evidence supporting the involvement of anti-Castro Cuban exiles will be examined in greater detail, shedding light on this compelling aspect of the assassination narrative.

Motives of Anti-Castro Cubans

The motives that might have driven anti-Castro Cuban exiles to participate in or even orchestrate the assassination of President John F. Kennedy stem from a deep sense of betrayal and frustration with the Kennedy administration's handling of Cuban affairs. These exiles, many of whom had fled their homeland after Fidel Castro's rise to power, harbored intense anger and resentment towards both Castro and the U.S. government, whom they felt had abandoned their cause.

The most significant catalyst for this resentment was the failed Bay of Pigs invasion in April 1961. The invasion, a covert operation planned by the CIA during the Eisenhower administration and inherited by Kennedy, aimed to overthrow Castro's regime by landing a force of Cuban exiles on Cuban shores. However, the operation was a disastrous failure. Despite initial planning and promises of support, Kennedy ultimately decided against providing the crucial air cover needed for the invading force to succeed. As a result, the invaders were quickly overwhelmed by Castro's forces, leading to significant casualties and the capture of many participants. This event was a profound blow to the Cuban exile community, many of whom had placed their hopes for a free Cuba on the success of the invasion.

In the aftermath of the Bay of Pigs, many Cuban exiles felt deeply betrayed by Kennedy. They believed that his refusal to provide adequate support during the invasion demonstrated a lack of commitment to their cause. This sense of betrayal was exacerbated by subsequent actions taken by the Kennedy administration, which appeared to signal a reluctance to engage in further direct military intervention against Castro's regime. Efforts to negotiate with the Soviet Union, including the Cuban Missile Crisis resolution in October 1962, which involved a U.S. pledge not to invade Cuba, further fueled the exiles' frustration and anger.

This seething discontent among the Cuban exile community created fertile ground for radical and desperate actions. For many exiles, the dream of returning to a free Cuba seemed increasingly remote under Kennedy's presidency. The perception that Kennedy's policies were not only ineffective but also actively hindering their cause led some to consider extreme measures, including assassination, as a means to instigate a change in U.S. policy.

Another motive for anti-Castro Cuban exiles to target Kennedy was the belief that his assassination could potentially lead to a more aggressive U.S. stance towards Castro's regime. Many exiles hoped that removing Kennedy from power might pave the way for a new administration that would take a harder line against Cuba, possibly resuming military efforts to overthrow Castro. This belief was not entirely unfounded, as many in the exile community had allies within the U.S. government and military who were sympathetic to their cause and shared their frustration with Kennedy's policies.

The assassination of President Kennedy, therefore, could be seen as a desperate act by a group that felt marginalized and betrayed by the very government they had once looked to for support. The exiles' desire for revenge against Kennedy, coupled with their hope for a renewed U.S. intervention in Cuba, provided a powerful motivation to participate in or support a plot to eliminate him.

As we continue to explore the involvement of anti-Castro Cuban exiles in the assassination, the next section will present the evidence that suggests their participation in this tragic event. By examining testimonies, connections, and circumstantial evidence, we can gain a deeper understanding of how these motives may have translated into action.

Evidence Supporting Their Involvement

As with any compelling conspiracy theory, the idea that anti-Castro Cuban exiles played a role in the assassination of President John F. Kennedy is supported by a patchwork of testimonies, connections, and circumstantial evidence. While definitive proof remains elusive, the accumulation of these pieces suggests a plausible narrative that warrants serious consideration.

One of the most significant pieces of evidence comes from the testimony of Silvia Odio, a Cuban exile living in Dallas. Odio claimed that in late September 1963, she was visited by three men, including Lee Harvey Oswald, who introduced himself as "Leon." According to Odio, the men identified themselves as members of an anti-Castro group and spoke disparagingly about President Kennedy. One of them reportedly said that "Leon" was "kind of loco" and capable of killing Kennedy. This encounter, if true, places Oswald in direct contact with anti-Castro elements just weeks before the assassination. Odio's testimony was considered credible by the House Select Committee on Assassinations (HSCA), which concluded that her account was persuasive and consistent with other evidence.

Further evidence comes from the activities and connections of individuals like David Ferrie and Guy Banister, both of whom had ties to anti-Castro Cuban groups and were connected to Oswald. Ferrie, a former airline pilot and associate of New Orleans Mafia boss Carlos Marcello, was also involved with Cuban exile activities. Banister, a former FBI agent turned private investigator, was known for his staunch anti-communist views and work with anti-Castro organizations. Oswald's association with Banister in New Orleans during the summer of 1963, where he was seen distributing pro-Castro leaflets, adds another layer of complexity to his political affiliations and potential involvement with anti-Castro elements.

The connections between anti-Castro Cubans and organized crime also bolster the theory of their involvement. Figures like Santo Trafficante Jr., the powerful boss of the Tampa crime family, had deep ties to both the Mafia and Cuban exile groups. Trafficante, who had significant investments in Cuban casinos before Castro's rise to power, was believed to be heavily involved in efforts to overthrow Castro. The intersection of organized crime interests and the anti-Castro cause creates a plausible scenario where these groups might have collaborated in a plot against Kennedy, whom they viewed as an obstacle to their objectives.

Another piece of the puzzle is the suspicious activity in Mexico City, where Oswald visited the Cuban and Soviet embassies in September 1963. While the purpose of his visit remains unclear, some theories suggest he might have been attempting to secure passage to Cuba or establish connections for a potential plot. The HSCA investigated these activities and found that Oswald's interactions in Mexico City could have involved anti-Castro Cuban elements working alongside intelligence operatives. This line of inquiry, though not conclusive, adds to the circumstantial evidence of a broader conspiracy involving Cuban exiles.

Finally, the testimonies of defectors and informants have provided additional insights. Several former Cuban exiles and intelligence operatives have come forward over the years, claiming to have knowledge of a plot involving anti-Castro groups. For example, a Cuban defector known as "Carlos" told the HSCA that anti-Castro exiles were involved in the assassination, motivated by a desire for revenge and a hope to reignite U.S. intervention in Cuba. Although these accounts are difficult to verify, they contribute to the larger body of evidence suggesting a Cuban exile connection.

In summary, the evidence supporting the involvement of anti-Castro Cuban exiles in the assassination of President Kennedy is multifaceted and complex. While it may not provide definitive proof, the combination of testimonies, connections, and suspicious activities paints a compelling picture of a possible conspiracy. As with other theories, the truth may lie in the interwoven threads of these various elements, demanding further investigation and a deeper understanding of the historical context.

Chapter 10: Other Powerful Groups

The Military-Industrial Complex

The theory that the military-industrial complex played a role in the assassination of President John F. Kennedy is one of the most pervasive and compelling conspiracies that has emerged over the decades. This theory is rooted in the intricate and often shadowy relationship between the U.S. government, the armed forces, and the defense contractors that supply them. At the heart of this theory are the substantial financial and strategic interests that were perceived to be threatened by Kennedy's policies and actions.

President Dwight D. Eisenhower famously warned of the potential dangers posed by the military-industrial complex in his farewell address in 1961. He cautioned that the conjunction of an immense military establishment and a large arms industry was new in the American experience and that its influence could endanger democratic processes. This prophetic warning set the stage for suspicions about the influence and motives of the military-industrial complex during Kennedy's presidency.

One of the primary motives attributed to the military-industrial complex is Kennedy's approach to the Vietnam War. While Kennedy initially increased U.S. involvement in Vietnam by sending military advisors and support, he became increasingly skeptical about the war's progression and the feasibility of a military victory. Reports and interviews with Kennedy's close aides suggest that he was considering a withdrawal of U.S. forces after the 1964 presidential election. This shift in policy posed a direct threat to the interests of defense contractors, who stood to lose billions of dollars from a de-escalation of the conflict. The loss of lucrative military contracts and the potential impact on the defense industry provided a powerful incentive for elements within the military-industrial complex to oppose Kennedy's policies.

Moreover, Kennedy's broader vision for U.S. foreign policy included a reduction in military expenditures and a focus on diplomatic solutions to global conflicts. His administration's efforts to negotiate arms control agreements with the Soviet Union, including the Partial Nuclear Test Ban Treaty of 1963, further alarmed hawkish elements within the military and defense sectors. These treaties aimed to limit the arms race and reduce the threat of nuclear war, but they also threatened the profitability of defense contractors who relied on a continuous demand for advanced weaponry and military technology.

Key figures within the defense industry and military leadership viewed Kennedy's policies as undermining national security and their financial interests. These individuals, often with close ties to defense contractors, had both the means and the motive to oppose Kennedy's administration. The convergence of military leaders with significant influence over national security policy and powerful defense contractors with vast resources created a potent force capable of orchestrating a conspiracy.

Evidence supporting this theory includes reports of suspicious activities and meetings among military and defense industry leaders in the months leading up to the assassination. For instance, there are accounts of high-level discussions about the potential impact of Kennedy's policies on the defense industry and the strategic direction of U.S. military engagements. Additionally, some researchers have pointed to anomalies in the security arrangements on the day of the assassination, suggesting possible complicity or at least knowledge within certain military circles.

While definitive proof of the military-industrial complex's involvement in Kennedy's assassination remains elusive, the convergence of motives, means, and opportunity creates a plausible narrative. The potential threat to the financial and strategic interests of the defense industry, combined with Kennedy's evolving policies, provides a compelling context for understanding why elements within this powerful group might have sought to remove him from office. As we continue to explore the various theories surrounding the assassination, the role of the military-industrial complex remains a critical and intriguing piece of the puzzle.

Oil Industry Moguls

Another group often implicated in the theories surrounding President Kennedy's assassination is the powerful oil industry moguls. The oil industry, with its significant economic influence and political connections, had substantial interests that could have been threatened by Kennedy's policies. The potential involvement of key figures within this sector offers a compelling narrative of how economic motives might have played a role in the events of November 22, 1963.

At the heart of this theory is the oil depletion allowance, a significant tax benefit that allowed oil companies to deduct a substantial portion of their income for tax purposes. This allowance was crucial for the profitability of oil companies, enabling them to retain more of their earnings and invest in further exploration and production. President Kennedy's tax reform initiatives, which aimed to close loopholes and increase tax revenues, threatened this lucrative benefit. The oil industry viewed these reforms as a direct attack on their financial interests.

Key figures in the oil industry, such as Clint Murchison and H.L. Hunt, are often mentioned in connection with this theory. Murchison, a Texas oil magnate, and Hunt, one of the wealthiest men in America at the time, had extensive political connections and were known for their right-wing views. Both men were vocal critics of Kennedy and his administration. Their influence extended beyond the oil industry into the realms of politics and intelligence, making them formidable opponents to any policy perceived as detrimental to their interests.

The connections between these oil moguls and political figures provide a network through which they could exert significant influence. For instance, Murchison and Hunt had strong ties to powerful politicians and former intelligence officials, creating a nexus of individuals who might have shared their concerns about Kennedy's policies. These relationships could have facilitated the planning and execution of a conspiracy to remove Kennedy from office.

Suspicious activities and meetings have been cited as evidence of the oil industry's involvement. One such event is the infamous "party" held at Clint Murchison's home in Dallas the night before the assassination. According to some accounts, this gathering included a who's who of powerful figures, including politicians, intelligence operatives, and business leaders. Among the attendees was reportedly J. Edgar Hoover, the FBI Director, who had long-standing ties to Murchison. The timing and nature of this meeting have fueled speculation that it was a planning session for the assassination.

Moreover, there are allegations that financial support for anti-Kennedy activities came from the oil industry. These claims suggest that substantial sums of money were funneled into efforts to undermine Kennedy's administration and promote opposition candidates who were more favorable to the interests of the oil magnates. The confluence of financial power and political influence created a potent force capable of orchestrating significant actions against perceived threats.

While definitive proof of direct involvement by oil industry moguls in Kennedy's assassination remains elusive, the circumstantial evidence and plausible motives suggest a scenario worth exploring. The convergence of economic interests threatened by Kennedy's policies and the capability of these powerful figures to influence political and intelligence operations creates a compelling narrative. As we continue to examine other groups potentially involved in the assassination, the role of the oil industry remains a critical component of the broader conspiracy theories.

This section seeks to contextualize the motives and connections of key oil industry figures, illustrating how their interests could align with the events leading up to and following the assassination. The intricate web of economic power, political influence, and covert operations underscores the complexity of the theories surrounding one of the most pivotal moments in American history.

Right-Wing Extremists

Among the myriad theories surrounding the assassination of President John F. Kennedy, the involvement of right-wing extremists is a significant and intriguing possibility. This theory posits that radical right-wing groups and individuals, vehemently opposed to Kennedy's policies and political ideology, may have played a role in the events of November 22, 1963. The potential motives, connections, and evidence associated with these extremists paint a compelling picture of ideological conflict and covert operations.

Right-wing extremism in the United States during the early 1960s was characterized by intense opposition to communism, civil rights advancements, and perceived federal overreach. Various far-right groups and individuals saw Kennedy's administration as a symbol of liberalism and a threat to their vision of America. The President's efforts to promote civil rights legislation, his cautious approach to the Cold War, and his perceived leniency towards the Soviet Union fueled their animosity.

One prominent group often linked to this theory is the John Birch Society. Founded in 1958 by businessman Robert Welch, the society was fiercely anti-communist and suspicious of any government action that seemed to align with communist interests. The John Birch Society viewed Kennedy's policies as dangerously progressive and part of a larger conspiracy to undermine American values and sovereignty. The society's publications and speeches frequently denounced Kennedy, portraying him as a traitor to the nation. While there is no direct evidence linking the John Birch Society to the assassination, the group's extreme rhetoric and widespread influence made it a focal point for right-wing extremist sentiment.

Another aspect of this theory involves individuals who were vocal and active opponents of Kennedy's policies. Figures such as General Edwin Walker, a staunch segregationist and anti-communist, epitomized the militant right-wing opposition. Walker had been relieved of his command by Kennedy in 1961 for distributing right-wing propaganda to his troops and subsequently became a vocal critic of the administration. Oswald's attempted assassination of Walker in April 1963, months before the Kennedy assassination, links Oswald to these ideological conflicts. Although Oswald's motives remain ambiguous, this connection highlights the volatile environment of the time.

Right-wing extremists also had substantial connections with influential political and business figures. Oil tycoons like H.L. Hunt, known for their far-right views and significant financial resources, were part of a network of individuals who opposed Kennedy. These connections provided both the means and the motive for orchestrating a high-level conspiracy. Meetings and communications among these figures often reflected a shared disdain for Kennedy and a desire to see his policies overturned.

Evidence supporting the involvement of right-wing extremists is largely circumstantial but compelling. Witnesses have reported seeing individuals known for their extremist views in Dallas around the time of the assassination. Additionally, the distribution of anti-Kennedy literature and the presence of inflammatory right-wing propaganda in the weeks leading up to the event suggest a coordinated effort to galvanize opposition to the President.

The potential involvement of right-wing extremists is further complicated by the political climate of the time. The 1960s were marked by significant social and political upheaval, with civil rights movements and anti-communist fervor often colliding. This environment of ideological extremism created a fertile ground for radical actions against perceived enemies.

In conclusion, the theory that right-wing extremists played a role in Kennedy's assassination reflects the broader societal tensions and conflicts of the era. While definitive evidence remains elusive, the combination of ideological motives, influential connections, and circumstantial evidence provides a plausible narrative. As we continue to explore the various dimensions of the conspiracy theories, the potential involvement of these radical elements highlights the complex and multifaceted nature of this enduring mystery.

Chapter 11: Declassified Documents and New Evidenc

Overview of Declassified Documents

The journey toward understanding the full scope of the assassination of President John F. Kennedy has been significantly shaped by the gradual release of declassified documents. These documents, previously hidden from public view, have provided critical insights and have fueled both scholarly research and conspiracy theories. The push for transparency began in earnest with the passage of the President John F. Kennedy Assassination Records Collection Act of 1992, which mandated the release of all government documents related to the assassination.

The National Archives and Records Administration (NARA) has played a pivotal role in this process, overseeing the declassification and release of millions of pages of documents. Among these are files from the CIA, FBI, Secret Service, and other government agencies. Each document offers a piece of the puzzle, contributing to a more comprehensive understanding of the events surrounding the assassination.

One of the most significant releases occurred in October 2017, when the National Archives made public thousands of previously classified documents. This release included detailed CIA and FBI files, internal government communications, and witness testimonies. Among the revelations were documents that shed light on Oswald's activities in Mexico City, where he visited the Soviet and Cuban embassies just weeks before the assassination. These files provided new context and raised further questions about Oswald's motivations and possible connections to foreign entities.

Another crucial set of documents released were those related to the House Select Committee on Assassinations (HSCA). Established in the late 1970s, the HSCA conducted a thorough reinvestigation of the assassination and concluded that there was a "high probability" of a conspiracy. The declassified HSCA records include interviews with key witnesses, forensic analyses, and discussions of various conspiracy theories. These documents have been instrumental in understanding the scope of the committee's work and the basis for their controversial conclusions.

The process of declassification has not been without its challenges. Despite the efforts mandated by the JFK Records Act, many documents remain heavily redacted or classified, citing national security concerns. The continued secrecy has fueled speculation and frustration among researchers and the public. Advocates for full transparency argue that the remaining documents could provide crucial insights and help resolve lingering questions about the assassination.

The impact of these declassified documents on public understanding and historical scholarship cannot be overstated. Each new release prompts a flurry of analysis and reexamination of existing narratives. Researchers pore over the documents, seeking connections, discrepancies, and new leads. These efforts have led to the discovery of previously unknown details, such as surveillance activities, covert operations, and internal disagreements within government agencies.

Furthermore, the declassified documents have played a pivotal role in keeping the assassination in the public consciousness. Media coverage of new document releases often brings the story back into the spotlight, prompting renewed interest and debate. Documentaries, books, and articles continue to explore the implications of these revelations, ensuring that the search for truth remains an ongoing process.

In summary, the declassification of documents related to the assassination of President Kennedy has been a crucial step in uncovering the full story. While many questions remain unanswered, the information that has emerged has enriched our understanding and provided a foundation for ongoing research and analysis. As we continue to sift through these records, the hope is that they will eventually lead to a more complete and accurate account of one of the most significant events in American history.

Impact on Conspiracy Theories

The release of declassified documents has had a profound impact on the landscape of conspiracy theories surrounding President Kennedy's assassination. Each new piece of evidence has the potential to either bolster existing theories or introduce entirely new lines of inquiry. As researchers and theorists delve into these documents, the complex web of narratives and speculations continues to evolve.

One of the most significant effects of these declassified documents has been the renewed scrutiny of the CIA's involvement. Documents have revealed extensive covert operations and surveillance activities that were previously unknown. For instance, files detailing the CIA's Project AMWORLD, which aimed to destabilize the Cuban government, have sparked debates about possible connections between these operations and the assassination. The timing of these covert actions and Oswald's interactions with pro-Castro groups have led some theorists to speculate that Oswald might have been manipulated or even directly involved in these clandestine efforts.

Similarly, the declassified files have shed new light on the FBI's role in the aftermath of the assassination. Documents reveal that J. Edgar Hoover, the FBI Director at the time, was adamant about establishing Oswald as the lone assassin, even before all the evidence had been thoroughly examined. This has raised questions about the integrity of the investigation and whether critical information was suppressed to fit a predetermined narrative. Such revelations have fueled theories that the FBI might have been complicit in a cover-up to protect broader government interests.

The Mafia's potential involvement has also been given new dimensions through declassified documents. Files indicating the extent of the Kennedy administration's crackdown on organized crime, and the subsequent animosity from figures like Carlos Marcello and Sam Giancana, have provided context for why the Mafia might have had a vested interest in eliminating Kennedy. Further, testimonies from mob informants and FBI surveillance records of mob communications have added credibility to claims of Mafia involvement, suggesting a complex interplay of motives and actions that intersect with the assassination plot.

The declassified documents have also had a significant impact on public perception and media coverage. News outlets often highlight the most sensational or controversial revelations, which can shape and sometimes skew public understanding. Documentaries and books based on newly released information frequently explore these findings, presenting them in ways that can support various conspiracy theories. This media portrayal helps keep the assassination and its mysteries alive in the public imagination, ensuring ongoing interest and debate.

Moreover, these documents have energized independent researchers and citizen investigators. The advent of the internet has made it easier for individuals to access, analyze, and share these declassified files. Online forums and communities dedicated to unraveling the mysteries of the Kennedy assassination have proliferated, with participants dissecting each new piece of evidence and debating its significance. This democratization of information has led to a more diverse array of theories and interpretations, each adding to the rich tapestry of the assassination's legacy.

In conclusion, the impact of declassified documents on conspiracy theories related to the JFK assassination has been substantial. They have provided new evidence and insights, challenged existing narratives, and fueled both scholarly research and public speculation. As more documents continue to be released, the landscape of conspiracy theories will undoubtedly continue to evolve, reflecting the enduring complexity and intrigue of one of the most pivotal moments in American history.

New Evidence and Its Implications

As researchers continue to delve into the trove of declassified documents related to President Kennedy's assassination, new evidence has emerged that further complicates and enriches our understanding of the event. These revelations, ranging from witness testimonies to forensic analyses and technological advancements, have provided fresh insights and raised additional questions about the official narrative and various conspiracy theories.

One of the most significant pieces of new evidence comes from advancements in forensic technology. Modern techniques in audio analysis, for example, have been applied to the infamous Dictabelt recording—a police radio transmission that some believe captured the sounds of the gunshots in Dealey Plaza. For decades, this recording has been at the center of debates, with some analysts asserting that it provides proof of multiple shooters. Recent re-examinations using sophisticated acoustic analysis have yielded mixed results, with some experts affirming the presence of multiple shots while others remain skeptical. These ongoing debates highlight the challenges of interpreting historical evidence with modern technology.

In addition to audio analysis, advances in digital imaging and photographic techniques have allowed researchers to re-examine key pieces of visual evidence. The Zapruder film, perhaps the most famous piece of evidence from the assassination, has been subjected to frame-by-frame digital enhancement, revealing details that were previously obscured. These enhancements have provided a clearer view of the sequence of events, though interpretations of what is seen in the frames continue to vary widely. Some analysts claim that the enhanced images support the theory of a second shooter, while others argue that they reinforce the lone gunman conclusion.

New witness testimonies have also emerged, shedding light on previously unexplored aspects of the assassination. For instance, several individuals who were reluctant to come forward at the time of the original investigation have since shared their accounts, adding new perspectives to the narrative. These testimonies, often recorded decades after the fact, must be carefully weighed against the potential for faded memories and the influence of existing conspiracy theories. Nonetheless, they provide valuable context and can corroborate or challenge other pieces of evidence.

The release of documents from foreign governments has further expanded the scope of available evidence. Countries such as Russia and Cuba have declassified their own files related to Oswald's activities and interactions with their embassies. These documents offer insights into how foreign intelligence agencies perceived and monitored Oswald, adding another layer of complexity to the investigation. For example, Russian files indicate that the KGB closely watched Oswald during his time in the Soviet Union but found him to be unstable and unreliable. Cuban documents, meanwhile, provide details of Oswald's visits to their embassy in Mexico City, suggesting that he was desperate to secure a visa to Cuba in the weeks before the assassination.

The implications of this new evidence are profound and multifaceted. Each revelation has the potential to support or undermine different aspects of the official narrative and various conspiracy theories. For instance, the enhanced forensic analyses and new witness testimonies may challenge the conclusions of the Warren Commission, suggesting that critical aspects of the investigation were either overlooked or misunderstood. Conversely, some new evidence may reinforce the idea that Oswald acted alone, providing further detail to his motivations and actions.

Verifying and integrating this new evidence into the broader historical context remains a significant challenge. Researchers must navigate a complex web of sources, each with its own biases and limitations. The process of sifting through mountains of data, cross-referencing testimonies, and applying modern forensic techniques requires a meticulous and balanced approach. Moreover, the passionate debate among scholars, theorists, and the public ensures that the quest for truth is ongoing and dynamic.

In conclusion, the continuous emergence of new evidence related to President Kennedy's assassination underscores the enduring complexity and intrigue of this historical event. As advancements in technology and new disclosures from various sources continue to add pieces to the puzzle, our understanding of the assassination evolves. While definitive answers may remain elusive, the pursuit of truth remains a vital and compelling endeavor, reflecting our collective desire to unravel the mysteries of one of the most pivotal moments in American history.

Chapter 12: The Impact on American Society

Cultural and Social Impact

CThe assassination of President John F. Kennedy on November 22, 1963, and the ensuing conspiracy theories have profoundly shaped American culture and society. This event, seared into the national consciousness, marked a turning point in how Americans view their government and the world around them. The cultural and social impacts of Kennedy's assassination are multifaceted, influencing public trust, media representations, and the collective memory of a generation.

One of the most significant cultural impacts of Kennedy's assassination has been the rise of skepticism and cynicism towards the government. The initial shock and horror of the event were soon followed by a growing mistrust of the official narrative presented by the Warren Commission, which concluded that Lee Harvey Oswald acted alone. As discrepancies and unanswered questions emerged, public faith in government transparency and competence began to erode. This skepticism was not confined to the assassination alone but extended to other aspects of governance and foreign policy, contributing to a broader sense of disillusionment.

The assassination also had a profound effect on American media and popular culture. The event and its aftermath have been depicted in numerous films, television shows, books, and other media, reflecting and shaping public perceptions over the decades. Films like Oliver Stone's "JFK" (1991) played a crucial role in bringing conspiracy theories to the forefront of popular discourse, blending fact and fiction to create a narrative that resonated with many viewers. These cultural representations have kept the assassination alive in the public imagination, continually reintroducing it to new generations and ensuring its place as a defining moment in American history.

Literature has also explored the themes of conspiracy and mistrust stemming from the Kennedy assassination. From Don DeLillo's novel "Libra" to Norman Mailer's "Oswald's Tale," authors have delved into the complexities of the event and its characters, providing nuanced interpretations that challenge official accounts. These literary works contribute to a rich tapestry of cultural reflection, inviting readers to question and ponder the broader implications of the assassination.

The collective memory of the Kennedy assassination has had a lasting impact on the generation that lived through it. For many, the event represents a loss of innocence and a moment when the idealism of the early 1960s gave way to a more turbulent and cynical era. The assassination became a touchstone for subsequent social and political movements, influencing the way Americans approached issues of civil rights, governance, and foreign policy. The sense of unresolved questions and the possibility of hidden truths fostered a climate of inquiry and skepticism that extended into other areas of public life.

The assassination also played a role in shaping subsequent social and political movements. The mistrust of government institutions that it engendered contributed to the anti-establishment sentiments of the late 1960s and 1970s, seen in movements such as the counter-culture, civil rights protests, and anti-Vietnam War demonstrations. These movements were driven by a desire for transparency, accountability, and social justice, reflecting the broader cultural shifts initiated by the shock of Kennedy's death.

In summary, the cultural and social impacts of the JFK assassination are profound and enduring. The event reshaped public trust, influenced media and literature, and left an indelible mark on the collective memory of a generation. As a defining moment in American history, the assassination continues to resonate, reflecting the complexities and challenges of understanding and interpreting a pivotal event that forever changed the nation's trajectory.

Political Ramifications

The assassination of President John F. Kennedy on November 22, 1963, sent shockwaves through the American political landscape, with repercussions that have echoed through the decades. The immediate and long-term political ramifications of the assassination were profound, influencing policy decisions, governmental reforms, and the overall trajectory of American politics.

One of the most immediate impacts of Kennedy's assassination was the abrupt transition of power. Vice President Lyndon B. Johnson was sworn in as President just hours after Kennedy's death, amid a climate of uncertainty and national mourning. Johnson's assumption of the presidency marked a significant shift in political priorities and style. While Kennedy had been a youthful, charismatic leader with a focus on idealism and progressive policies, Johnson brought a pragmatic and forceful approach to the office. This transition facilitated the passage of several key legislative initiatives, most notably the Civil Rights Act of 1964 and the Voting Rights Act of 1965, which were significant milestones in the American civil rights movement.

The assassination also led to increased security measures for public officials, particularly the President. The Secret Service underwent significant reforms, with enhanced protocols to ensure the safety of the President during public appearances. These changes included improved communication systems, more rigorous background checks, and greater collaboration with local law enforcement agencies. The tragic event underscored the vulnerabilities in the protection of high-profile political figures and prompted a comprehensive overhaul of security practices.

Kennedy's death and the subsequent investigation by the Warren Commission had lasting implications for governmental transparency and accountability. The Warren Commission, tasked with investigating the assassination, concluded that Lee Harvey Oswald acted alone. However, the Commission's findings were met with skepticism and criticism, leading to widespread debate and distrust. The perceived inadequacies of the investigation and the lack of transparency fueled numerous conspiracy theories, which questioned the Commission's conclusions and suggested possible cover-ups.

This growing mistrust in the government prompted further inquiries and investigations. In the late 1970s, the House Select Committee on Assassinations (HSCA) re-examined the evidence and concluded that there was a high probability of a conspiracy. The HSCA's findings, while not definitively proving any particular theory, suggested that the Warren Commission's investigation had overlooked crucial evidence and raised questions about the thoroughness and integrity of the initial inquiry. This re-examination reinforced the need for greater governmental transparency and accountability, leading to subsequent reforms in how sensitive investigations were conducted and reported.

The assassination also influenced the course of American foreign policy. Kennedy's vision of détente and his efforts to ease tensions with the Soviet Union were cut short by his untimely death. Johnson, while continuing some aspects of Kennedy's foreign policy, adopted a more aggressive stance in Vietnam, leading to a significant escalation of U.S. involvement in the conflict. The Vietnam War, in turn, had profound effects on American politics and society, contributing to widespread protest and political polarization. The war's divisive nature underscored the complexities of foreign policy decisions and their far-reaching consequences.

The political ramifications of Kennedy's assassination extended to the electoral process as well. The event highlighted the importance of vice-presidential selection and the need for continuity of leadership in the face of unforeseen tragedies. It also influenced the strategies and platforms of subsequent presidential candidates, who sought to address the concerns and anxieties of a public still reeling from the shock of Kennedy's death. The legacy of the assassination shaped political discourse, emphasizing themes of security, accountability, and the search for truth.

In summary, the assassination of President Kennedy had profound political ramifications that shaped the course of American history. It led to significant legislative achievements, prompted reforms in security and investigative practices, and influenced foreign and domestic policy decisions. The enduring legacy of the assassination continues to impact American politics, reflecting the complexities and challenges of navigating a nation's response to a pivotal and tragic event.

Enduring Legacy and Ongoing Debates

The assassination of President John F. Kennedy remains one of the most scrutinized and debated events in American history. Its enduring legacy is not only reflected in the countless investigations and conspiracy theories but also in the ongoing engagement of new generations of researchers and the public. The assassination's impact on American society has continued to evolve, driven by the release of new evidence, technological advancements, and the ever-present quest for truth.

The enduring legacy of the JFK assassination is evident in how it has permeated American identity and historical narrative. For many, it symbolizes a moment when trust in government began to wane, marking the start of an era characterized by skepticism and a demand for transparency. The assassination challenged the nation's belief in the infallibility of its institutions and leaders, fostering a culture of inquiry and doubt that persists to this day.

Over the decades, the release of declassified documents and new evidence has fueled ongoing debates and research. Each revelation has prompted reexaminations of the official narrative and has spurred further investigation into alternative theories. The internet has played a crucial role in this process, providing a platform for researchers to share information, collaborate, and debate their findings. Online forums, social media platforms, and dedicated websites have created a space where the public can engage with the complexities of the assassination, ensuring that the quest for understanding remains vibrant and dynamic.

One of the most significant aspects of the assassination's legacy is its impact on the field of historical and forensic research. The continuous emergence of new evidence has pushed the boundaries of investigative techniques and forensic science. Researchers have utilized advancements in technology, such as enhanced imaging and audio analysis, to reexamine key pieces of evidence. These technological innovations have provided new perspectives and have challenged previous conclusions, highlighting the evolving nature of historical inquiry.

The assassination has also influenced popular culture, keeping the event in the public consciousness through films, documentaries, books, and other media. Works such as Oliver Stone's "JFK" and numerous investigative books have played a significant role in shaping public perceptions and keeping the debates alive. These cultural representations not only reflect the ongoing fascination with the assassination but also contribute to the collective memory and understanding of the event.

Moreover, the assassination has inspired a dedicated community of independent researchers and citizen investigators. These individuals, often referred to as "citizen historians," have made significant contributions to the body of knowledge surrounding the assassination. Their work, driven by a passionate pursuit of truth, exemplifies the democratization of historical research in the digital age. By meticulously analyzing documents, conducting interviews, and collaborating with other researchers, these citizen historians continue to unearth new insights and challenge established narratives.

The quest for answers has also led to the establishment of various investigatory bodies, such as the Warren Commission and the House Select Committee on Assassinations. While their conclusions have been the subject of intense debate and criticism, these efforts reflect the importance of institutional responses to public demand for accountability and transparency. The ongoing efforts to release all related documents underscore the belief that the public has a right to know the full truth about the assassination.

In conclusion, the assassination of President John F. Kennedy has left an indelible mark on American society. Its legacy endures through the ongoing debates, research, and cultural representations that continue to shape public understanding. As new generations engage with the complexities of the event, the quest for truth and closure remains a powerful and unifying force. The assassination stands as a testament to the enduring impact of historical events on national identity and the collective consciousness, reflecting the perpetual human desire to seek answers and understand the past.

Chapter 13: Modern Investigations and Technology

Advances in Forensic Technology

The assassination of President John F. Kennedy has been one of the most analyzed events in modern history, with each new generation of investigators applying the latest forensic technologies in hopes of uncovering new insights. Over the past few decades, significant advancements in forensic science have revolutionized the field, allowing for a more detailed and nuanced re-examination of the evidence surrounding Kennedy's death.

One of the most transformative technologies has been digital imaging. High-resolution scans and digital enhancement techniques have provided clearer, more detailed views of key pieces of evidence, such as the Zapruder film. This home movie, captured by Abraham Zapruder, remains one of the most critical pieces of visual evidence, documenting the assassination in real-time. Modern digital imaging allows for frame-by-frame analysis, revealing details that were previously obscured or overlooked. Enhanced images have provided new perspectives on the timing and sequence of shots, the movements of the people in Dealey Plaza, and the interactions between Kennedy and his surroundings. This technology has not only reinforced certain aspects of the official narrative but has also fueled ongoing debates about the presence of additional shooters and the exact trajectory of the bullets.

Another significant advancement has been in the field of 3D modeling and reconstruction. Using laser scanning and photogrammetry, forensic experts have created highly accurate, three-dimensional models of Dealey Plaza and the Texas School Book Depository. These models allow investigators to simulate the assassination from various angles, providing a more comprehensive understanding of the spatial relationships and potential lines of sight. By recreating the positions of Kennedy, the motorcade, and the suspected shooting locations, researchers can test different scenarios and theories with a high degree of precision. This technology has been instrumental in examining the plausibility of the "grassy knoll" theory and other alternative viewpoints.

Enhanced audio analysis has also played a crucial role in modern investigations. The Dictabelt recording, a police motorcycle radio transmission that some believe captured the sounds of the gunshots, has been subjected to sophisticated acoustic analysis. Advanced techniques, such as waveform analysis and sound spectrum analysis, have been used to scrutinize the recording for patterns and anomalies. While interpretations of the Dictabelt remain contested, these analyses have provided valuable data on the number and timing of the shots, contributing to the ongoing debate about the possibility of multiple shooters.

In addition to visual and audio technologies, advancements in material science and forensic ballistics have provided new insights into the physical evidence. Techniques such as neutron activation analysis and scanning electron microscopy allow for detailed examination of bullet fragments, determining their composition and origin with greater accuracy. These methods have been applied to the bullets and bullet fragments recovered from the assassination, offering a more precise understanding of their trajectories and the wounds they caused. This level of detail has been crucial in assessing the validity of the single bullet theory, also known as the "magic bullet" theory, which posits that one bullet caused multiple wounds in both President Kennedy and Governor John Connally.

The application of these advanced forensic technologies has not only deepened our understanding of the Kennedy assassination but has also highlighted the complexities and challenges of historical investigations. Each new methodology brings its own set of insights and limitations, contributing to a more nuanced and multi-faceted picture of the events of November 22, 1963. As technology continues to evolve, so too will our ability to explore and interpret the evidence, keeping the quest for truth alive and ongoing.

Re-examination of Physical Evidence

The re-examination of physical evidence using contemporary methodologies has provided significant new insights into the assassination of President John F. Kennedy. Modern forensic techniques have allowed researchers to scrutinize the ballistic evidence, medical reports, and autopsy findings with a level of detail that was not possible at the time of the original investigation.

One of the primary focuses of re-examination has been the ballistic evidence, particularly the analysis of bullet trajectories and impacts. The bullets and fragments recovered from the assassination scene and the victims have been subjected to advanced forensic techniques, such as neutron activation analysis and scanning electron microscopy. These methods enable forensic scientists to determine the elemental composition of the bullet fragments with high precision, allowing for a more accurate assessment of their origins and trajectories.

The single bullet theory, which posits that a single bullet caused multiple wounds in both President Kennedy and Governor John

Connally, has been a central point of contention since the Warren Commission's report. Modern forensic analyses have re-evaluated this theory by examining the physical properties of the bullets and the nature of the wounds. For instance, 3D modeling and ballistic simulations have been used to recreate the trajectories and impacts, providing a more detailed understanding of how a single bullet could have caused such extensive damage. These analyses have offered support for the single bullet theory by demonstrating that the trajectory and behavior of the bullet are consistent with the wounds observed in both Kennedy and Connally. However, some researchers continue to challenge this theory, arguing that the complexity of the injuries suggests the involvement of multiple shooters.

The re-evaluation of medical and autopsy reports with modern medical knowledge and technology has also been a crucial aspect of the investigation. The original autopsy, conducted under less-than-ideal conditions and with limited expertise in forensic pathology, has been the subject of much criticism. Modern forensic pathologists have re-examined the autopsy photographs, X-rays, and reports, using contemporary medical standards and advanced imaging techniques to provide a clearer picture of the injuries sustained by Kennedy.

Digital enhancements of the autopsy photographs and X-rays have allowed for a more accurate assessment of the entry and exit wounds, as well as the trajectory of the bullets. These enhancements have helped clarify some of the ambiguities and discrepancies in the original autopsy findings. For example, the re-examination has provided a better understanding of the head wound and the direction of the fatal shot. By aligning the medical evidence with the ballistic analyses, modern forensic experts have been able to corroborate or challenge previous conclusions, contributing to a more comprehensive understanding of the assassination.

In addition to the ballistic and medical evidence, the physical locations and environmental factors have also been re-examined. Advanced technologies, such as laser scanning and 3D reconstruction, have been used to create accurate models of Dealey Plaza and the Texas School Book Depository. These models allow investigators to analyze the spatial relationships and potential lines of sight with greater precision. By simulating the positions of the motorcade, the shooters, and the surrounding environment, researchers can test various scenarios and theories to determine their plausibility.

These re-examinations of physical evidence using modern methodologies have provided valuable insights and have either reinforced or challenged existing theories about the assassination. The meticulous analysis and re-evaluation of the evidence have highlighted the complexities of the case and the importance of using advanced forensic techniques to uncover the truth. As technology continues to evolve, so too will our ability to re-examine historical events with greater accuracy and detail, ensuring that the quest for understanding the assassination of President Kennedy remains a dynamic and ongoing process.

New Investigative Approaches and Their Findings

The relentless pursuit of understanding the assassination of President John F. Kennedy has led investigators to embrace innovative methodologies and cutting-edge technologies. These new investigative approaches have provided fresh perspectives and have shed light on longstanding questions, contributing significantly to the body of knowledge surrounding this historic event.

One of the most groundbreaking developments in modern investigative techniques is the use of computer simulations and artificial intelligence (AI). Advanced computational models allow researchers to recreate the assassination in meticulous detail, analyzing various scenarios to test their plausibility. For example, researchers have developed sophisticated 3D simulations of Dealey Plaza, integrating all available data on the positions of the motorcade, the locations of witnesses, and the trajectories of the bullets. These simulations can be manipulated to explore different angles and potential shooting positions, providing a dynamic tool for analyzing the event. By simulating the assassination, investigators can better understand the mechanics of the shots fired, the timing of the events, and the possible presence of additional shooters.

AI and machine learning algorithms have also been employed to analyze vast amounts of data related to the assassination. These technologies can sift through thousands of documents, photographs, and audio recordings to identify patterns and correlations that might have been missed by human researchers. For instance, AI algorithms can analyze the contents of declassified documents, cross-referencing names, dates, and locations to uncover connections and inconsistencies. This automated approach has the potential to reveal new insights and to corroborate or challenge existing theories, making it an invaluable tool in the ongoing investigation.

Another innovative approach involves the use of forensic audio and video enhancement technologies. High-resolution audio analysis tools have been applied to recordings from the assassination, such as the Dallas police radio transmissions and other contemporary audio sources. These tools can filter out background noise, isolate specific sounds, and enhance the clarity of the recordings, providing a more detailed and accurate audio landscape of the event. Similarly, video enhancement technologies have been used to improve the quality of existing footage, such as the Zapruder film, allowing for more precise analysis of the visual evidence. By applying these advanced techniques, researchers can gain new insights into the timing and sequence of the shots, the reactions of witnesses, and other critical aspects of the assassination.

Recent investigations have also benefited from advancements in forensic anthropology and pathology. Modern forensic techniques, such as digital autopsy and 3D imaging, have been used to re-evaluate the medical evidence related to Kennedy's wounds. Digital autopsy software allows forensic pathologists to create virtual reconstructions of the president's injuries, providing a detailed and interactive model for analysis. This approach has helped clarify the nature of the wounds and the trajectories of the bullets, supporting or challenging previous conclusions. Additionally, forensic anthropologists have re-examined the physical evidence with a focus on biomechanical analysis, exploring how the human body reacts to gunshot trauma. These studies provide a deeper understanding of the effects of the bullets and the potential implications for the single bullet theory.

The findings from these new investigative approaches have had significant implications for our understanding of the assassination. In some cases, they have reinforced the conclusions of previous investigations, providing additional evidence to support the lone gunman theory or other aspects of the official narrative. In other instances, they have introduced new questions and possibilities, suggesting alternative scenarios and highlighting areas where further research is needed. The application of modern technologies and methodologies continues to push the boundaries of what we know about the assassination, ensuring that the quest for truth remains an evolving and dynamic process.

In summary, the use of advanced investigative approaches, such as computer simulations, AI, and forensic enhancement technologies, has provided invaluable insights into the assassination of President Kennedy. These methodologies have allowed researchers to re-examine the evidence with unprecedented detail and precision, uncovering new information and challenging existing theories. As technology continues to advance, the investigation into Kennedy's assassination will undoubtedly continue to evolve, bringing us closer to a comprehensive understanding of this pivotal moment in American history.

Chapter 14: Conclusion

Summation of Evidence and Arguments

The assassination of President John F. Kennedy remains one of the most complex and debated events in American history. Throughout this book, we have explored a myriad of theories and evidence, each contributing to a multifaceted understanding of what transpired on November 22, 1963. This section aims to synthesize the key findings and arguments presented, offering a cohesive overview of the investigation's most compelling aspects.

From the outset, the official narrative presented by the Warren Commission has been scrutinized and challenged by a plethora of alternative theories. The Commission's conclusion that Lee Harvey Oswald acted alone in assassinating President Kennedy has faced persistent skepticism, fueled by inconsistencies and gaps in the evidence. Our exploration began with an in-depth analysis of Oswald's background, motivations, and potential connections to various groups. The enigmatic nature of Oswald's life, from his defection to the Soviet Union to his pro-Castro activities, provided fertile ground for speculation about his true role and affiliations.

The examination of potential government involvement revealed a complex interplay of motives and actions. Theories suggesting the involvement of the CIA and FBI were bolstered by declassified documents and testimonies that exposed covert operations and surveillance activities. The rapid destruction of evidence and the swift conclusion drawn by the FBI further fueled suspicions of a cover-up. The role of key figures such as J. Edgar Hoover and the possible manipulation of the investigation by higher-ups highlighted the potential for institutional bias and protection of broader interests.

The possible involvement of organized crime, particularly the Mafia, emerged as a compelling theory supported by substantial evidence. The Kennedys' aggressive crackdown on organized crime, led by Attorney General Robert F. Kennedy, provided a strong motive for Mafia figures like Carlos Marcello, Sam Giancana, and Santo Trafficante to conspire against the President. Testimonies from mob informants, connections between Oswald and Mafia associates, and suspicious activities surrounding key individuals painted a vivid picture of a possible criminal conspiracy.

Anti-Castro Cuban exiles also featured prominently in the investigation. Their deep resentment towards Kennedy, stemming from the failed Bay of Pigs invasion and perceived abandonment by the U.S. government, provided a plausible motive for their involvement. Connections between Oswald and Cuban exile groups, as well as testimonies from individuals like Silvia Odio, suggested a potential link between these exiles and the assassination plot.

The exploration of other powerful groups, such as the military-industrial complex, oil industry moguls, and right-wing extremists, further expanded the scope of potential conspirators. Each of these groups had distinct motives rooted in economic, political, or ideological interests. The intersections of these interests with the actions and policies of the Kennedy administration provided a rich context for understanding the broader implications of the assassination.

Modern forensic technology and contemporary methodologies have played a crucial role in re-examining the evidence. Advances in digital imaging, 3D modeling, audio analysis, and forensic pathology have provided new insights and clarified previous ambiguities. These technologies have enabled a more precise analysis of key pieces of evidence, such as the Zapruder film, Dictabelt recording, and ballistic trajectories. While some findings have reinforced the official narrative, others have introduced new questions and possibilities, underscoring the complexity of the case.

In conclusion, the synthesis of evidence and arguments presented in this book illustrates the multifaceted nature of the JFK assassination. The interplay of various motives, actions, and interests has created a tapestry of intrigue and mystery that continues to captivate researchers and the public alike. As we delve deeper into the remaining mysteries and the enduring impact of the assassination, it becomes clear that the quest for truth is both a historical and a cultural endeavor, reflecting our collective desire to understand one of America's most pivotal moments.

Remaining Mysteries

Despite extensive investigations and countless theories, many aspects of President John F. Kennedy's assassination remain unresolved and contentious. These lingering mysteries continue to fuel debate among researchers, historians, and the public, highlighting the complexities and enduring intrigue of this pivotal event.

One of the most persistent questions revolves around the possibility of multiple shooters. The official narrative, as presented by the Warren Commission, concluded that Lee Harvey Oswald acted alone. However, numerous eyewitness testimonies and independent analyses suggest otherwise. Many witnesses reported hearing shots coming from different directions, particularly the infamous "grassy knoll" area in Dealey Plaza. Acoustic evidence, including the controversial Dictabelt recording, has been interpreted by some experts as indicating multiple gunshots from different locations. Despite modern forensic re-examinations and simulations, the debate over the number of shooters remains a core mystery, with no definitive resolution.

Another area of contention is the true extent of government involvement, or at the very least, the possibility of a cover-up. Declassified documents and testimonies have revealed significant surveillance and covert operations by the CIA and FBI, which have led some researchers to suspect these agencies' deeper involvement. The rapid destruction of evidence, such as the cleaning of the presidential limousine and the handling of Oswald's interrogation, has only added to the suspicions. The reluctance of certain government officials to release all related documents further fuels the theory that crucial information is being withheld from the public. The question of whether key figures within the government were complicit in either the assassination itself or in obstructing the truth remains a tantalizing enigma.

The motivations behind key actions on the day of the assassination also continue to puzzle investigators. For instance, the behavior of Lee Harvey Oswald, both before and after the assassination, is riddled with inconsistencies and unexplained actions. Oswald's connections to various groups, his defection to the Soviet Union, and his pro-Castro activities create a convoluted web of affiliations that complicate understanding his true motives. Similarly, the actions of Jack Ruby, who killed Oswald two days after the assassination, raise questions about whether he acted independently or was part of a larger conspiracy. Ruby's known connections to organized crime and his erratic behavior have led to numerous theories about his true purpose in silencing Oswald.

The physical evidence also presents its own set of unresolved questions. The infamous "single bullet theory" proposed by the Warren Commission remains highly debated. Critics argue that the trajectory and damage attributed to the single bullet defy the laws of physics, suggesting the involvement of additional shooters. Modern forensic analyses and 3D reconstructions have provided conflicting interpretations, leaving this theory as one of the most hotly contested aspects of the case. Additionally, the precise nature of Kennedy's head wounds and the direction of the fatal shot have been subjects of ongoing debate, with different medical experts offering varying opinions.

The passage of time has only added to the complexities of achieving a definitive conclusion. As key witnesses and individuals directly involved in the investigation pass away, the opportunity to obtain firsthand accounts diminishes. Furthermore, the remaining classified documents and the potential loss or destruction of critical evidence over the years create additional hurdles for researchers.

In summary, the assassination of President Kennedy remains shrouded in mystery, with many questions still unanswered. The possibility of multiple shooters, the extent of government involvement, the motivations behind key actions, and the interpretation of physical evidence continue to fuel debates and investigations. These enduring mysteries highlight the challenges of uncovering the full truth about a complex historical event, reflecting the persistent quest for understanding and the human desire to resolve unanswered questions. As new evidence and technologies emerge, the investigation into Kennedy's assassination will undoubtedly continue, driven by the hope of one day achieving clarity and closure.

Enduring Impact on Public Trust

The assassination of President John F. Kennedy has had a profound and lasting impact on public trust in government institutions. This tragic event, coupled with the numerous conspiracy theories that have emerged over the decades, has shaped public perceptions of transparency, accountability, and integrity in ways that continue to resonate in American society.

In the immediate aftermath of the assassination, the American public was plunged into a state of shock and mourning. President Kennedy had been a symbol of youthful optimism and progressive ideals, and his sudden death left a void that was difficult to fill. As the initial grief gave way to questions and doubts, the Warren Commission was established to investigate the assassination. While the Commission's intent was to provide clarity and closure, its findings—that Lee Harvey Oswald acted alone—were met with widespread skepticism. Discrepancies in the evidence, conflicting testimonies, and perceived gaps in the investigation fueled doubts about the official narrative.

This skepticism was compounded by subsequent revelations of covert government activities and internal documents that painted a picture of potential malfeasance and cover-ups. The release of declassified documents over the years has only added to the complexity, revealing information that has both supported and contradicted various aspects of the official story. As a result, the perception that the government was either incapable of or unwilling to reveal the full truth took root in the collective consciousness.

The erosion of trust was not confined to the Kennedy assassination alone. The event set a precedent for how the American public viewed subsequent governmental actions and investigations. The Vietnam War, Watergate scandal, and other political controversies of the 1960s and 1970s further exacerbated this mistrust. The belief that the government could—and sometimes did—engage in deceptive practices became more entrenched, leading to a broader cultural cynicism towards political institutions and leaders.

The enduring impact of the assassination on public trust is also evident in the rise of conspiracy culture. The Kennedy assassination became a foundational event for the proliferation of conspiracy theories, which questioned not only the specifics of the assassination but also the broader motives and actions of those in power. This culture of suspicion has permeated various aspects of American life, influencing how citizens interpret political events, media reports, and official statements. The notion that hidden forces operate behind the scenes, manipulating outcomes for their own benefit, has become a persistent theme in American discourse.

In addition to fostering a culture of skepticism, the assassination has had significant implications for the way historical events are studied and understood. The quest for truth and accountability has driven countless researchers, historians, and citizen investigators to delve into the minutiae of the event, scrutinizing every piece of evidence and exploring every possible theory. This ongoing investigation reflects a deep-seated desire for transparency and justice, highlighting the importance of open access to information and the need for rigorous, unbiased inquiry.

The lessons learned from the Kennedy assassination underscore the critical importance of maintaining public trust in government institutions. Transparency, accountability, and clear communication are essential components of a healthy democracy. The enduring questions and unresolved aspects of the assassination serve as a reminder of the consequences when trust is eroded and information is withheld. Ensuring that the public feels confident in the integrity of governmental processes and investigations is vital for the stability and cohesion of society.

In conclusion, the assassination of President Kennedy has left an indelible mark on public trust in government. The event and its surrounding theories have shaped perceptions of transparency and accountability, fostering a culture of skepticism that persists to this day. As we reflect on the enduring impact of the assassination, it is clear that the quest for truth and the need for trust in governmental institutions remain as relevant and crucial as ever. The legacy of the Kennedy assassination continues to influence American society, reminding us of the importance of vigilance and integrity in the face of complex and consequential historical events.

Chapter 15: Further Reading and Resources

Books and Scholarly Works
For readers who wish to delve deeper into the complexities and enduring questions surrounding the assassination of President John F. Kennedy, a wealth of books and scholarly works offers comprehensive analyses, varied perspectives, and detailed investigations. This curated list includes both seminal texts and recent publications that have significantly contributed to the field.

1. Gerald Posner, "Case Closed: Lee Harvey Oswald and the Assassination of JFK" Gerald Posner's "Case Closed" is a meticulous examination of the evidence, making a compelling argument that Lee Harvey Oswald acted alone. Posner's work is noted for its detailed forensic analysis and extensive interviews, providing a thorough rebuttal to many conspiracy theories. The book is an essential read for those seeking a comprehensive understanding of the official narrative.

2. Vincent Bugliosi, "Reclaiming History: The Assassination of President John F. Kennedy" Vincent Bugliosi's magnum opus, "Reclaiming History," spans over 1,600 pages and is one of the most exhaustive studies of the assassination. Bugliosi, a former prosecutor, meticulously dissects conspiracy theories, presenting a robust defense of the Warren Commission's findings. This book is a crucial resource for readers interested in a detailed legal and investigative perspective.

3. James W. Douglass, "JFK and the Unspeakable: Why He Died and Why It Matters" James W. Douglass offers a profound and thought-provoking exploration of the motives and forces that may have led to Kennedy's assassination. Douglass's narrative is deeply critical of the official account, positing that powerful elements within the U.S. government and military-industrial complex orchestrated the assassination. This book is essential for readers interested in a moral and philosophical inquiry into the assassination.

4. David Lifton, "Best Evidence: Disguise and Deception in the Assassination of John F. Kennedy" David Lifton's "Best Evidence" presents a controversial yet intriguing hypothesis that the medical evidence related to Kennedy's wounds was tampered with. Lifton's detailed analysis of the autopsy and medical reports provides a unique perspective on potential cover-ups. His work is significant for those exploring the intricacies of the medical evidence.

5. Anthony Summers, "Not in Your Lifetime: The Defining Book on the JFK Assassination" Anthony Summers' "Not in Your Lifetime" is a critical investigation that synthesizes decades of research and new evidence. Summers examines various conspiracy theories and evaluates the plausibility of different scenarios, offering a balanced and insightful narrative. This book is a valuable resource for readers seeking a comprehensive overview of the ongoing debate.

6. Lamar Waldron and Thom Hartmann, "Ultimate Sacrifice: John and Robert Kennedy, the Plan for a Coup in Cuba, and the Murder of JFK" Lamar Waldron and Thom Hartmann delve into the connection between Kennedy's assassination and secret plans for a coup in Cuba. Their research uncovers new evidence and connections, providing a fresh perspective on the motives and players involved. This book is an essential read for those interested in the geopolitical dimensions of the assassination.

These books represent a broad spectrum of perspectives and methodologies, offering readers a comprehensive foundation for understanding the complexities of the JFK assassination. Whether seeking to confirm the official narrative or explore alternative theories, these scholarly works provide invaluable insights into one of the most enduring mysteries of the 20th century.

Documentaries and Films

The Kennedy assassination has been a source of intrigue and debate for decades, inspiring a wealth of documentaries and feature films that provide visual and narrative examinations of the events surrounding the fateful day. This section delves into some of the most notable works, highlighting their unique perspectives, contributions, and impact on public perception.

Key Documentaries

One of the seminal works in this genre is "The Men Who Killed Kennedy," a compelling series that explores various conspiracy theories and the numerous individuals who might have been involved. This documentary offers a detailed investigation into alternative explanations, making it a must-watch for those who question the official account.

Another significant documentary is "JFK: The Smoking Gun." This film presents a controversial theory suggesting that a Secret Service agent accidentally fired the fatal shot. Through meticulous research and forensic analysis, "JFK: The Smoking Gun" challenges conventional narratives and introduces new evidence that has sparked further discussion and debate.

Notable Feature Films

Oliver Stone's "JFK" stands out as a cornerstone of cinematic portrayals of the Kennedy assassination. This feature film, starring

Kevin Costner as New Orleans District Attorney Jim Garrison, delves deep into the conspiracy theories and governmental cover-ups. Stone's meticulous attention to detail and dramatic storytelling have left an indelible mark on the public's understanding and interest in the assassination.

"JFK" is not merely a film; it's a cultural phenomenon that re-ignited public scrutiny and dialogue about the assassination. Its narrative weaves together various theories, presenting a thought-provoking and sometimes controversial view that continues to resonate with audiences.

Impact and Importance

These documentaries and films play a crucial role in shaping public perception and keeping the conversation about the Kennedy assassination alive. They provide visual and narrative complements to written resources, catering to those who prefer multimedia approaches to learning. Each work offers a distinct lens through which to examine the events, encouraging viewers to question, analyze, and engage with history.

By presenting these key documentaries and films, we aim to enrich your understanding of the Kennedy assassination, offering diverse perspectives that contribute to the ongoing dialogue. Whether you're a seasoned researcher or a curious newcomer, these visual works are invaluable resources for exploring one of the most significant and debated events in American history.

Articles and Online Resources

In an era where information is at our fingertips, the wealth of articles and online resources available on the Kennedy assassination has never been more accessible or comprehensive. This section aims to guide readers through the maze of digital resources, highlighting key articles, online archives, and websites that provide up-to-date and reliable information.

Reputable Online Archives

One of the most valuable resources is the JFK Assassination Records Collection, housed by the National Archives. This extensive archive offers a treasure trove of primary documents, including official government reports, witness testimonies, and declassified files. Researchers and history enthusiasts alike can delve into these original sources to gain a deeper understanding of the events and controversies surrounding the assassination.

Scholarly Articles

For those seeking rigorous academic analyses, scholarly articles from journals such as The Journal of American History are indispensable. These peer-reviewed publications offer expert insights and meticulously researched studies that shed light on various aspects of the Kennedy assassination. By engaging with this scholarship, readers can explore different interpretive frameworks and evaluate the evidence with a critical eye.

Trusted Websites

In addition to archives and academic journals, there are several trusted websites dedicated to assassination research. Websites like the Mary Ferrell Foundation provide comprehensive databases, expert analyses, and forums for community discussion. These platforms offer a space for researchers and enthusiasts to share findings, debate theories, and stay informed about the latest developments in the field.

Another essential resource is the Assassination Archives and Research Center, which offers a wide range of documents and analyses. This site serves as a hub for researchers and historians, providing access to valuable materials and fostering a collaborative environment for ongoing study.

The Value of Online Resources

The availability of these online resources ensures that anyone interested in the Kennedy assassination has the tools to stay informed and engaged. Primary documents offer firsthand accounts and evidence, while expert analyses provide context and interpretation. Community discussion platforms allow for the exchange of ideas and the exploration of new perspectives.

By utilizing these articles and online resources, readers can continue to learn and contribute to the evolving dialogue about one of the most significant events in American history. Whether you're a seasoned researcher or a curious newcomer, these digital tools offer invaluable support for your journey into the mysteries of the Kennedy assassination.

Chapter 16: Appendix

Point 1: Critical Documents

Outline:

- **Introduction to Key Documents**: Overview of why these documents are crucial to the narrative.
- **Government Reports and Official Documents**: Detailed references to government-issued reports, such as the Warren Commission Report and other official investigations.
- **Declassified Files**: Highlighting recently declassified documents and their impact on our understanding of the assassination.
- **Eyewitness Testimonies and Affidavits**: A collection of firsthand accounts that provide unique perspectives on the events surrounding the assassination.
- **Analysis and Commentary**: Summarizing expert analyses and interpretations of these documents.

Point 2: Interviews

Outline:

- **Introduction to Interviews**: Explanation of the significance of interviews in providing personal insights and firsthand accounts.
- **Notable Interviews with Key Figures**: Transcripts and summaries of interviews with important figures directly involved in or affected by the assassination.
- **Journalist and Investigator Interviews**: Including interviews with journalists and investigators who have dedicated their careers to uncovering the truth.
- **Impactful Interviews from Documentaries and Films**: Key interviews featured in documentaries and films discussed in Section 2, providing additional context and depth.
- **Reflections and Analyses**: Expert reflections on the interviews and their contributions to the overall understanding of the assassination.

Point 3: Primary Sources
Outline:

- **Introduction to Primary Sources**: Importance of primary sources in historical research and their role in this book.
- **Archival Photographs and Videos**: Collection of significant photographs and videos from the period, with descriptions and analyses.
- **Letters and Correspondence**: Important letters and correspondence between key figures, providing insight into their thoughts and actions.
- **Contemporaneous News Articles and Media Coverage**: Selection of contemporary news articles and media reports that shaped public perception at the time.

- **Document Analysis**: Techniques for analyzing primary sources and how they were used to construct the narrative in this book.

Critical Documents

The assassination of President John F. Kennedy has generated a vast array of documents that are crucial for understanding the intricacies of the event. These documents provide direct insights into the investigation processes, the official conclusions, and the multitude of theories that have emerged over the years. This section compiles and presents the most critical documents referenced throughout this book, allowing readers to examine the primary sources firsthand.

Government Reports and Official Documents

1. **The Warren Commission Report**: Officially known as "The Report of the President's Commission on the Assassination of President Kennedy," this extensive document details the findings of the Warren Commission, which concluded that Lee Harvey Oswald acted alone in the assassination. The report is essential for understanding the official narrative and the evidence that supported the Commission's conclusions.

2. **The House Select Committee on Assassinations Report (HSCA)**: Conducted in the late 1970s, the HSCA investigation revisited the Kennedy assassination and concluded that there was a "probable conspiracy." This report offers an alternative perspective to the Warren Commission, highlighting the possibility of additional conspirators and new evidence that had emerged since the original investigation.

3. **The FBI's Records and Files**: The Federal Bureau of Investigation conducted its own investigation into the assassination, paralleling the efforts of the Warren Commission. The FBI's

records include investigative reports, witness statements, and internal communications that provide a comprehensive view of the agency's findings and the methods used to gather evidence.

Declassified Files

1. **CIA Documents**: The Central Intelligence Agency has released numerous documents related to the assassination, including files on Lee Harvey Oswald's activities, surveillance reports, and internal communications. These declassified documents offer a glimpse into the CIA's operations and its role in the broader context of the Cold War.
2. **National Security Agency (NSA) Files**: NSA records include intercepted communications and intelligence reports that were pertinent to the investigation. These documents provide valuable information on the international implications of the assassination and the various geopolitical factors at play.

Eyewitness Testimonies and Affidavits

1. **Testimonies from Dealey Plaza Witnesses**: The accounts of individuals who were present in Dealey Plaza on the day of the assassination are invaluable. These testimonies offer firsthand perspectives on the sequence of events, the sounds of the gunshots, and the reactions of those in the vicinity.
2. **Affidavits of Key Figures**: Affidavits from important figures, such as law enforcement officers, medical personnel, and government officials, provide detailed accounts of their actions and observations. These documents help piece together

the timeline of events and clarify the roles played by various individuals.

Analysis and Commentary

1. **Expert Analyses of Key Documents**: Throughout this book, various experts have provided analyses and interpretations of the critical documents. These commentaries offer context, highlight significant findings, and address discrepancies or ambiguities within the primary sources.
2. **Historical and Contemporary Perspectives**: The documents compiled in this section are accompanied by historical and contemporary perspectives that explore their significance and impact. By examining these documents in detail, readers can gain a deeper understanding of the evidence and arguments that have shaped the ongoing discourse around the Kennedy assassination.

The compilation of these critical documents in the appendix serves as a valuable resource for readers who wish to engage directly with the primary sources. By providing access to these foundational materials, this section enables a comprehensive and informed exploration of one of the most significant events in American history.

Interviews

Interviews are a cornerstone of historical research, offering invaluable firsthand accounts and personal insights that enrich our understanding of events. The assassination of President John F. Kennedy is no exception, and this section compiles some of the most impactful and revealing interviews conducted over the years. These interviews provide perspectives from those directly involved in or affected by the assassination, as well as from investigators and journalists who have dedicated their careers to uncovering the truth.

Notable Interviews with Key Figures

1. **Lee Harvey Oswald's Interrogations**: Although no recordings of Oswald's interrogations survive, transcripts and notes taken by Dallas police officers and FBI agents provide a glimpse into Oswald's demeanor and responses during the critical hours following his arrest. These documents reveal his denials of guilt and his claim of being a "patsy," which have fueled numerous conspiracy theories.

2. **Jack Ruby's Jailhouse Interviews**: After killing Oswald, Jack Ruby granted several interviews to law enforcement officials and journalists. Ruby's statements have been scrutinized for clues about his motives and potential connections to larger conspiracies. These interviews are essential for understanding Ruby's state of mind and the circumstances that led to his dramatic act.

3. **Interviews with First Lady Jacqueline Kennedy**: Jacqueline Kennedy's interviews, particularly those conducted by historian Arthur Schlesinger Jr., offer a deeply personal perspective on the events surrounding her husband's assassination. Her reflections on the day of the assassination and its aftermath provide emotional and poignant insights into the impact on the Kennedy family.

Journalist and Investigator Interviews

1. **Jim Garrison's Interviews**: As the New Orleans District Attorney who famously prosecuted Clay Shaw, Jim Garrison's interviews are a crucial resource for understanding the investi-

gation that inspired Oliver Stone's film "JFK." Garrison's discussions about his theories and the evidence he uncovered provide a detailed look at one of the most controversial legal proceedings related to the assassination.

2. **Interviews with Gerald Posner**: Author of "Case Closed," Gerald Posner has conducted numerous interviews explaining his exhaustive research that supports the lone gunman theory. Posner's discussions offer a thorough analysis of the evidence and counterarguments to various conspiracy theories.

3. **Researchers and Historians**: Interviews with prominent researchers and historians, such as David Lifton, Anthony Summers, and James W. Douglass, provide diverse perspectives on the assassination. These experts discuss their findings, methodologies, and the challenges they faced in their investigations, offering valuable context and depth to their written works.

Impactful Interviews from Documentaries and Films

1. **Oliver Stone's "JFK" Interviews**: The film "JFK" features interviews with key figures, such as Jim Garrison and witnesses from Dealey Plaza. These interviews, conducted during the making of the film, highlight the different theories and controversies surrounding the assassination, and have had a lasting impact on public perception.

2. **"The Men Who Killed Kennedy" Interviews**: This documentary series includes interviews with a wide range of individuals, from eyewitnesses to conspiracy theorists. The series' comprehensive approach and the diversity of its interviewees provide a broad spectrum of views and information.

3. **"JFK: The Smoking Gun" Interviews**: Featuring interviews with forensic experts and investigators, this documentary presents a controversial theory about a possible accidental shot fired by a Secret Service agent. The interviews offer detailed forensic analyses and alternative viewpoints that challenge conventional narratives.

Reflections and Analyses

1. **Expert Reflections on Interviews**: Throughout this book, experts have analyzed and reflected on the interviews presented here. Their commentaries provide critical insights into the reliability and significance of the interviewees' statements, helping to piece together a more coherent and nuanced understanding of the assassination.

2. **Historical Context**: Placing these interviews within the broader historical context is essential for appreciating their full significance. The reflections on these interviews help to contextualize the events and the personal experiences of those involved, providing a richer narrative of the assassination and its aftermath.

This compilation of interviews serves as a crucial resource for readers seeking to understand the Kennedy assassination through the voices of those who lived it and those who have dedicated their lives to investigating it. By presenting these firsthand accounts, this section offers a deeper, more personal connection to the historical events and ongoing debates.

Primary Sources

Primary sources are the bedrock of historical research, offering firsthand accounts and direct evidence of past events. In the case of

President John F. Kennedy's assassination, these sources are invaluable for constructing a detailed and accurate narrative. This section compiles the most critical primary sources referenced throughout this book, providing readers with direct access to the documents, photographs, and media that form the foundation of our understanding.

Archival Photographs and Videos

1. **The Zapruder Film**: Perhaps the most famous piece of visual evidence, the Zapruder film is a 26-second home movie captured by Abraham Zapruder, which recorded the assassination in real-time. This film has been meticulously analyzed for decades and remains a central piece of evidence in understanding the sequence of events. The frames of this film are available through various archives, including the National Archives and the Sixth Floor Museum at Dealey Plaza.

2. **Other Photographs from Dealey Plaza**: Numerous photographs taken by bystanders and professional photographers on the day of the assassination provide multiple perspectives of the event. Key images include those taken by Mary Moorman, which capture the motorcade at the moment of the fatal shot, and by James Altgens, a press photographer whose images offer a broader view of the plaza and the immediate aftermath.

3. **News Footage and Broadcasts**: Live television and radio broadcasts from November 22, 1963, provide real-time reactions and reporting from the scene. News footage from stations such as CBS and NBC captures the chaos and confusion that followed the shooting, as well as the official announcements of President Kennedy's death.

Letters and Correspondence

1. **Lee Harvey Oswald's Letters**: The personal letters of Lee Harvey Oswald, including those sent to his family and Soviet officials, offer insights into his state of mind and ideological motivations. These letters have been used to trace Oswald's movements and to understand his connections to various political groups.

2. **Government Correspondence**: Official correspondence between various government agencies, such as the FBI, CIA, and Secret Service, provides a detailed account of the investigation's progress and the internal deliberations that took place. These letters reveal the complexities and challenges faced by investigators and decision-makers in the aftermath of the assassination.

Contemporaneous News Articles and Media Coverage

1. **The Dallas Morning News**: Local newspapers, such as The Dallas Morning News, provide detailed accounts of the events as they unfolded. Articles from November 23, 1963, and the following days offer contemporary perspectives and report on the public's reaction, the investigation's early stages, and the emerging theories.

2. **The New York Times and The Washington Post**: National newspapers covered the assassination extensively, with in-depth reporting on the investigation, the political implications, and the broader impact on American society. These articles are essential for understanding the media landscape and public discourse during this critical period.

3. **Life Magazine**: Known for its impactful photojournalism, Life Magazine published several special issues dedicated to the Kennedy assassination. These issues include some of the most iconic images and comprehensive coverage of the event and its aftermath.

Document Analysis

1. **Techniques for Analyzing Primary Sources**: Understanding how to analyze primary sources is crucial for historical research. Techniques such as cross-referencing documents, assessing the credibility of sources, and contextualizing information within the broader historical framework are essential for constructing a reliable narrative.

2. **Applying Analysis to the JFK Assassination**: This section includes examples of how primary sources were analyzed to draw conclusions about the assassination. By examining specific documents, photographs, and media reports, readers can see the methodologies used to piece together the events of November 22, 1963.

By compiling these primary sources, this section of the appendix provides readers with the tools to explore the JFK assassination in-depth. These documents, photographs, and media reports are not only vital for historical accuracy but also for fostering a deeper understanding of one of the most significant and scrutinized events in American history.